BEAUFORT
NORTH CAROLINA

The Beaufort waterfront and Inlet Inn boardwalk, c. 1890.

THE
MAKING OF AMERICA
SERIES

BEAUFORT
NORTH CAROLINA

MAMRÉ MARSH WILSON
AND BEAUFORT HISTORICAL ASSOCIATION

ARCADIA
PUBLISHING

Published by Arcadia Publishing
Charleston, South Carolina

Printed in the United States of America

Library of Congress control number: 2001092154

For all general information contact Arcadia Publishing at:
Telephone 843-853-2070
Fax 843-853-0044
E-Mail sales@arcadiapublishing.com
For customer service and orders:
Toll-Free 1-888-313-2665

Visit us on the Internet at www.arcadiapublishing.com

DEDICATED TO A LOVER OF KNOWLEDGE AND HISTORY

JIM HOWLAND

APRIL 16, 2002

CONTENTS

ACKNOWLEDGMENTS

The first to be acknowledged for the production of this volume are the explorers and discoverers who put their lives in the hands of the captains of the sea to sail to the new world.

Second, the government of Great Britain is to be acknowledged for having the foresight to allow Raleigh the opportunities he had to settle along the coast of what has become North Carolina.

Third, acknowledgement must be made to the Jamestown settlement as well, as many of those who left Virginia for the undeveloped, dangerous, water-bound area of the northeastern portion of North Carolina were the progenitors of the settlers in Beaufort and Carteret County.

A fourth thank-you goes to the people who were willing to put their lives on the line to plan and establish the town of Beaufort and to their descendants who have continued to make the area their home.

And finally, in the twentieth century, there are many who have written about the delightful town by the sea, promoting tourism and life at the water's edge. Among them are the authors of booklets and brochures in the early years, writers and historians Jean Bruyere Kell, Charles Paul, Peter Sandbeck, Maurice Davis, and others who have provided information through the Carteret Historical Research Association and their two volumes of family history, *The Heritage of Carteret County*, as well as Ruth Peeling Barbour, who has written about the formation of the Beaufort Historical Association.

Also, Jane Wolff, the public information officer of the North Carolina Maritime Museum of Beaufort; *The Gam*, a local newspaper, for printing the "Beaufort Scrapbook" authored by Nancy Russell, with wonderful stories of her memories of growing up in Beaufort; Ashley Sullivan and others who audio-taped several family histories; and Peggy Langdale, who as a volunteer with the Beaufort Historical Association spent months videotaping interviews of local citizens and their stories.

A History of North Carolina used in the public schools many years ago; *The Ashe History of North Carolina*; William P. Cumming; Samuel Eliot Morison; Mary Lynn Bryan, editor of the Jane Addams Papers; as well as the Carteret County Register of Deeds office; the Carteret County Public Library; the State of North

Carolina Department of Cultural Resources; and many more—too numerous to name—have provided the resources for research and authorship.

Acknowledgement must also be given to the many friends who have encouraged me over the years to learn more about this special place, especially John Costlow and Jim Howland, with whom discussions have gone long into the evenings. I also thank God for the gifts he has given me and the strength and courage to complete this task.

Lastly, I must acknowledge the publishers of this volume, and editors Mark Berry and Jim Kempert, for their interest in doing the Making of America series and inviting former authors to participate.

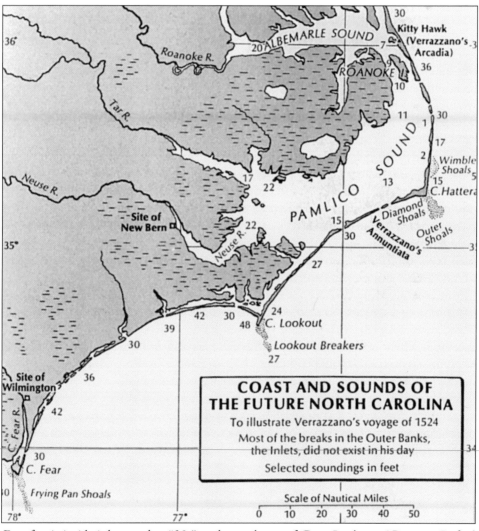

COAST AND SOUNDS OF THE FUTURE NORTH CAROLINA

To illustrate Verrazzano's voyage of 1524

Most of the breaks in the Outer Banks, the Inlets, did not exist in his day

Selected soundings in feet

Scale of Nautical Miles

Beaufort is inside inlet number "30," to the northwest of Cape Lookout. (Courtesy Oxford University Press.)

PREFACE

Imagine:

You are young, inquisitive, and you know that there is more to the world than what you have grown up surrounded by in Europe. You set off to see what's on the other side of that great water that moves constantly along your shore. It's a small but sturdy boat with lots of sail and plenty of work to keep you busy, both mind and body. By evening each day you begin to wonder what you have gotten yourself into. Will you ever see land again? What will it look like? You have left all the known for the unknown.

Many days after facing the raging sea, the storms, the heat, and even the calms when the ship doesn't go anywhere, someone yells that there is land in the distance. From that moment on the trip was worth it. Without even going ashore, you can see and smell the wonders of the new land you have found. There are people there, but no great houses or streets like those you left behind. There is wonderful sea life and beautiful trees along a shoreline that is gently washed by the ocean. Amazingly, there is even an ocean on the other side of the narrow strip of land. What stories you can tell when you return home!

You have lived in the new land for several months, met the natives, learned some of their ways, and even appear to have made friends. But there is something beneath the obvious that makes you wonder if you really are welcome here. You and others who sailed across the sea, leaving behind all you have ever known—civilization, wonderful cities, big handsome houses, comfort—are now in a place where there is nothing except what you make of it.

You build places to sleep and eat, nothing like what you had before, and you even build a fort around your small houses and gardens, to keep the animals from wandering away and becoming lost in that great wilderness. But even with all that, there is still a curiousness of the unknown. What is beyond? Where does that river go? Can you cross this wide expanse of water and find more land? Would new areas be nicer, more habitable, less populated by the natives?

After sailing south for days, following the shoreline, you and your fellow travelers discover that there is a body of water that grows narrower the farther you go. You eventually appear to be going to the west. There is smoke in the distance. More of the natives, you imagine. Are they friendly? Will they share with you?

An aerial view of the inlet leading to Beaufort and Morehead City, c. 1971.

This is a beautiful setting. There are wonderful trees, a beautiful shoreline, and even sand banks that protect the land and waters, which would be a great harbor for larger ships.

When you return to your home in the northeastern part of the country, where there is now government, civilization, beautiful homes, churches, family and friends, you plan your next trip to that new-found place just to the south. With the local surveyor you plot the land, lay off acreage, patent it for yourself or the King, and eventually decide to attempt a settlement there. It is not easy starting over. The natives are not as friendly as those you left behind: they seem to be determined to make you leave. After all, you have taken their land and waters, and are a threat to their existence.

But you persevere and eventually set up a small village on that narrow bit of water, displacing the natives who have been sent to another part of the country after they waged war against you. Life is good along the shore. Some of your group have built large homes along the waterfront, while the rest live in smaller houses similar to those you saw on some of the islands you visited on your voyage to this new land.

Over the years you share your new-found land with pirates who love to enter the safe harbor for food and water. You stave off attacks by the Spanish and French and even by your former homeland. There is rumbling and rumor of separation from England where your ancestors and families lived. Why not separate? You

John White's 1585 map of Virginia showing some of the sea life explorers encountered. (Courtesy NC Department of Cultural Resources, Division of Archives and History.)

have your own government, your own laws and courts, you are free here to live and worship as you wish.

You are now an American. You live in a place called Beaufort in the county of Carteret in the state of North Carolina. Life is good here. There are more and more people moving into your community, some coming to help build the new fort that is going up on the banks across the inlet from town. People are buying lots in town, paying taxes, running for office. There are police and even a small fire brigade. Your children are growing up in the safety and beauty of this place.

Then you hear rumors of secession. Some people want to leave the northern part of America because you have slaves, and the northerners don't like that. Your new president wants you to stay together as one country. Citizens are divided. You watch as some of the residents row across the inlet and take over the fort from the Union man and his family who are caring for it.

Then there is the news that your country is at war with itself. What a tragedy: families divided, brothers fighting brothers, women left to take care of the home, some even becoming spies. You see the Northern army take over the town, move into the grand houses, use your harbor as a refueling station. It's amazing, you think: They are just like you are, only from a different part of the country and talking in a different language almost, and they seem to like you.

At the end of the battles and after the surrender, some of the "yankees" stay around and help you get things back together. They even begin teaching your now-freed slaves how to read and write, and all about various trades so that they can live with their freedom. Life is different now. You sense there is a newness in the community. It is a new time.

You have seen war, you have lived with reconstruction, you have seen the beginning of the new century. There are bigger ships fishing off the banks, there are strange, noisy cars driving along your streets, there is even a railroad approaching across the waters of the river. New buildings are going up and there is another war, although this time it is back in the old countries. Life moves along slowly here in Beaufort. You are now a twentieth-century American, a North Carolinian, and you see the changes taking place in your home town and county.

New people move in again, more homes are built, roads are paved, there are more cars, the train arrives daily bringing tourists to stay at the inns and homes, and life is exciting. Soon, the face of Beaufort changes. You are no longer the longtime resident who settled the area many centuries before. The people living here are now from all parts of the country, seeking the peace and beauty that you once sought. Old buildings are torn down to make way for modern structures. The waterfront is alive with fancy yachts and powerful ships now, but there are also sailboats making their way south or north, some not so different from the one that first brought you here.

You have come full circle, but there is much more that you cannot even imagine.

THE HISTORY

In writing the history of Beaufort, it is impossible to do so without telling the stories of those who explored the coast of America, discovered the capes and outer banks of North Carolina, attempted settlements in the late 1500s, and eventually found the area known today as Carteret County, establishing the port town of Beaufort.

The story begins in the early 1500s with the adventures of Verrazzano and other explorers and continues through the Raleigh expeditions and the Lost Colony, the establishment in the 1600s of Lords Proprietors to govern the new-found land of the Carolinas, and the eventual settlement of Beaufort and the surrounding communities, particularly down east, in the early 1700s.

I have found in my 30 years of living in Beaufort and doing research that this is a family community where heritage means a lot. It is made up of the descendants of those who came to the area seeking new opportunities and freedom to live as they desired. They came with the courage to establish homes surrounded by woods and water, with nothing but good soil to grow their farms, fish and wildlife to maintain their bodies, and the power of their faith to sustain their souls.

Not everyone survived the difficulty of living among natives who were unhappy about the encroachment of the white man. At times friends and family of the settlers were attacked and killed, but those who managed to live through the hard times made a difference in the lives of everyone. There were fishermen, farmers, carpenters, tailors, shoemakers, blacksmiths, innkeepers, joyners, surveyors, shipwrights, and mariners.

It took those who worked the land and the waters, built the homes, made the clothing, and planted and reaped the crops to make a living for everyone. Some became justices of the court, commissioners of the town, vestrymen of the parish, and even held high offices in the government of the province.

But it is the families and their descendants that settled, lived, raised children and grandchildren, and died here that have made Beaufort the unique community it has been for the last 400 years.

It is an honor to share some of these people and their families with you.

A late-sixteenth century copy of a Florentine portrait of Giovanni da Verrazzano. (Courtesy Oxford University Press.)

1. THE DISCOVERERS

The east coast of today's United States had never been mapped by Europeans until the early 1500s. Giovanni da Verrazzano was born in 1485 in Tuscany, south of Florence, to wealthy parents. He became a mathematician and at age 20–21 he moved to Dieppe, in the maritime section of Normandy, to pursue a maritime career. Dieppe had deep water and a harbor. Verrazzano sailed on many voyages, including ones to Newfoundland, Carthage, and Damascus, and he was a friend of Magellan at Seville before Magellan made his voyage around the world in 1517.

In 1523, at age 38, Verrazzano had an impeccable maritime record and as an Italian mariner appealed to King Francis I of France. Italian bankers living in Lyons, France appointed Verrazzano as commander of an armada to sail west in search of a strait or passage from the Atlantic Ocean to the east coast of China.

His ship *La Dauphine*, built in La Havre in 1519 for the Royal Navy, was 100 tons with a crew of 50. The voyage began with four ships including one called *La Normande* and two that were lost early in a tempest. Prior to beginning the long voyage they took prizes along the coast and *La Normande* escorted them to France. *La Dauphine* alone sailed to the new world.

Verrazzano kept a journal in which he recorded the latitude and longitude of the various places he visited. His plan was to sail parallel to the Columbus voyage several years earlier; however, he chose to set off on 32° 30' north latitude. On January 17, 1524 he said farewell to the old world, but one week later ran into the worst tempest he had ever experienced and altered his course to west by north, and turned west at 34° north latitude. On or about March 1 he made landfall near Cape Fear at latitude 33° 50' 47" north. Cape Fear is the southernmost of the three North Carolina capes. The dangerous and nearly hidden Frying Pan Shoals extend out to sea 15 miles there. The other capes, Lookout and Hatteras, also have shoals that cause captains to shudder and keep from coming near shore.

Verrazzano did not stay in the Cape Fear region long. Since he was forced to take a more northern latitude crossing the Atlantic, he missed exploring the southern coast. Therefore, before heading north he sailed south 50 leagues (a league being about 3.5 miles), or about 175 miles. At this point he decided to turn north again to avoid the Spanish who were in the Florida area. Verrazzano returned to Cape Fear and anchored offshore.

He and some of his crew went ashore in a small boat and met the natives. Verrazzano described them as being russet, with hair black and thick that they tied together in a knot in the back and wore like a ponytail. They were well formed in their limbs, average in stature, although somewhat bigger than the crew, broad-breasted, with strong arms. Their bodies did not appear to be disfigured, he reported. Some had eyes wide apart that were great and black. They had a cheerful and steady look. According to Verrazzano, these natives were not strong, but were sharp-witted and nimble, being great runners.

Heading back to his ship, Verrazzano continued northward, anchored, and took note of the sand dunes fronted with upland palmettos and bay bushes. The cypresses, he wrote, smelled so sweet even far from shore. On March 25 he sailed north-northeast and anchored again offshore, in the open. He sent a boat ashore, but the area was so rough with waves continually pounding the beach that they could not land.

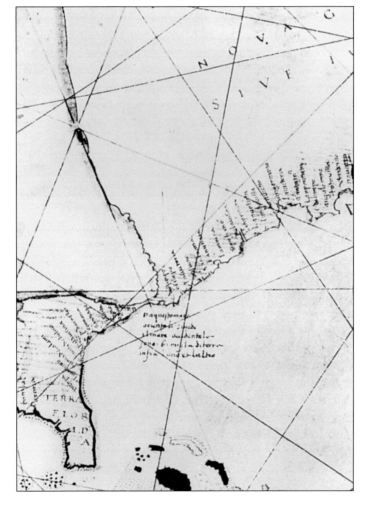

Gerolamo da Verrazzano's 1529 map of the new world.

He decided to send one of his crew swimming with several "gifts" for the natives who were standing on shore watching all this. The young man nearly drowned, but the Indians took care of him. They warmed him, dressed him in dry clothes, and sent him back. According to his description, the natives were "inclining to black as the others were with their flesh shining, average stature, handsome visage, delicate limbs with very little strength, but a prompt wit."

Two historians have their own ideas on where this occurred along the coast of Carolina. In *The European Discovery of America, The Northern Voyages,* A.D. *500–1600,* Samuel Eliot Morison states that the area is possibly on the Outer Banks between Cape Lookout and Cape Hatteras, or even a bit north of Hatteras. He notes that Verrazzano had found "an isthmus a mile in width and about 200 long, in which, from the ship, we could see el mare orientale, halfway between West and North," which he named Verrazzania. Continuing, Verrazzano states "We sailed along this isthmus in continual hope of finding some strait or northern promontory at which land would come to an end, in order to penetrate to quelli felici liti del Catay" (those happy shores of Cathay, meaning China).

On the other hand, in *Mapping the North Carolina Coast, Sixteenth-Century Cartography and the Roanoke Voyages,* William P. Cumming's comment on this event says it occurred while they were sailing east along the North Carolina barrier islands between Cape Fear and Cape Lookout. He says Verrazzano rounded Cape Lookout and sailed along the Outer Banks, where he made his geographical mistake of thinking he had found el mare orientale. As the date was March 25, he named the area Annunciata in honor of the Annunciation of the Virgin.

Cumming also cites Verrazzano's comments that Annunciata was the country around Cape Lookout and that the length of the Outer Banks from Cape Lookout to Old Currituck Inlet is 190 miles.

Morison writes that following Annunciata, *La Dauphine* sailed 50 leagues, or 175 miles, to a place he called Arcadia because of the beauty and tall trees. Morison says that this area could be none but the area near Nags Head, Kitty Hawk, and Kill Devil Hills. They anchored April 10 and remained three days.

Again Verrazzano described the natives of Arcadia as being "handsome, naked, hair fastened in a knot, and of olive color." They wore leaves for clothes and fished or fowled. This time he described their canoes, the grapevines, flowers, and herbs that were different from those of the old country. On today's maps, Arcadia has moved more eastward and become L'Acadie, the French name for Nova Scotia, New Brunswick, and part of Maine.

Cumming states that Verrazzano followed the coast, which "veered somewhat to the north" (perhaps Cape Hatteras) and "after 50 leagues [175 miles] reached another land full of great forests." It appears that this is the same area written about by Morison, for Cumming too mentions the encounter with the Native Americans. Cumming adds, however, a description of the women with some children hiding in the grass, and the fact that the sailors took an 8-year-old boy and carried him back to France. Cumming says these incidents in Arcadia could have taken place anywhere between Cape Lookout and the Delaware River.

It was Verrazzano's written report of July 8, 1524, and the maps drawn by his brother Gerolamo that influenced the great English exploration of the same area of the coast of North Carolina. In 1582, Richard Hakluyt translated the Italian version into English and published it in his *Divers Voyages*. Thus it was made available to those planning the Raleigh voyages.

Maps of the time show two prominent projections on the Atlantic coast between Florida and Newfoundland: Cabo de Trafalgar (Cape Lookout) and Cabo de las Arenas (Cape Cod). One mapmaker gave the latitude of Trafalgar as 35.5° north, one degree too high for Cape Lookout and Beaufort, which are located at 34° 37' 19" latitude and 76° 30' 41" longitude.

The English planners of overseas ventures, including Sir Humphrey Gilbert, Richard Hakluyt, and Sir Walter Raleigh, used many of these maps in charting their voyages to the New World.

A detail of the east coast of North America from the anonymous "Harleian" world map, c. 1547.

2. THE RALEIGH VOYAGES

Anyone living along the coast of North Carolina has almost certainly heard of Sir Walter Raleigh and the Lost Colony of Roanoke. Raleigh was born in 1552 to Walter and Katherine Raleigh. His half brother Sir Humphrey Gilbert, son of Katherine and Otho Gilbert, was born in 1539. Together these brothers were adventurous seekers of what lay beyond their shores, and they loved the sea.

Raleigh was with his brother on Gilbert's voyage to the Nova Scotia area as captain of the ship *Falcon*. A second voyage in 1583 ended in the death of Gilbert. It was then that Raleigh made his decision to follow through on a plan that Gilbert had to plant a colony in North America. A patent was issued March 25, 1584 and Raleigh received the same vice regal powers that Gilbert had had, authority over all in the colony. He was warned, however, that no plundering at sea or on land would be allowed. The penalty for such actions was to pay restitution or, if unable, the colony would be turned loose from the protection and care of England!

The first of Raleigh's adventures was in 1584, the second in 1585–1586, the third in 1587–1589, and the fourth in 1590. The area of present-day Beaufort was the scene of many of them.

THE FIRST VOYAGE: 1584

The first voyage was planned using Richard Hakluyt's translation of Verrazzano's report of 1524. From April to September 1584, Philip Amadas and Arthur Barlow, with Simon Ferdinando as their flag pilot, explored the coast of the new world, scouting for an area where a colony could be settled. Amadas at the time was only 20, and with Barlow had been in the household of Raleigh in London and Devonshire.

On April 27, 1584, Amadas (commanding the flagship), Arthur Barlow (commanding the second bark), and Simon Ferdinando left Plymouth, England. They arrived in the Canary Islands in mid-May and in June came upon the West Indies. On June 22 they left Cuba and entered the Gulf Stream, and by July 2 were off the coast of Georgia. With the moon at first quarter on July 4 they sighted land midway between Cape Fear and Cape Lookout. For the next nine days they sailed along the Carolina coast.

Sir Humphrey Gilbert, from a contemporary portrait at Compton Castle. (Courtesy Oxford University Press.)

No inlet was found until full moon on July 13 after they had sailed approximately 120 miles. This inlet, according to historian Samuel Eliot Morison, has since disappeared and been replaced by Oregon Inlet; however, the area where the inlet and islands were located appears to have been Hatteras Island, which is south of Oregon Inlet today.

The islands on either side were heavily wooded and inhabited by the Algonquin Indians. The entrance was shallow, only about 12 feet of water at high tide, so the crew anchored on the southern side and using small boats, they went ashore and took possession for "the Queen's most excellent Maiestie." A description says the island was low and sandy, full of summer grapes, with cedar, pine, cypress, sassafras, tupelo, and other trees.

On the third day contact was made with the natives and gifts of food and clothing were exchanged. The tribe was called Roanoke from the island of the same name. They were described as being very handsome and goodly people with behavior as mannerly as any of the people of Europe. The soil was plentiful and sweet and as fruitful as anywhere in the world. Winters were never hard or cold and in summer the islands were cooled by a sea breeze.

During their stay in this area, Barlowe and others sailed in the ship's longboat 20 miles up the Albemarle Sound and River, and on their way back stopped and visited the Roanoke village on Roanoke Island. Barlowe commented that he "found the people most gentle, loving and faithful, void of all guile and treason." They had yellowish skin and black hair, although some of the children appeared to have fine auburn and chestnut hair.

As they were preparing to depart, two Native Americans, Manteo and Wanchese, volunteered to accompany them home. They sailed on August 23 and arrived in England on September 15.

THE SECOND VOYAGE: 1585–1586

By spring 1585 Raleigh had been knighted, becoming Sir Walter Raleigh. His seal showed his arms with the motto of "Amore et Virtute!" An inscription described it as the insignia of Walter Raleigh, Knight, Lord and Governor of Virginia.

When he planned his second voyage, it was made clear to him by Queen Elizabeth that he was *not* to be on board. She would help him by loaning him a ship of the Royal Navy, the *Tiger*, and giving him £400 worth of powder from the royal magazine, but he was to remain in England. In fact, she gave him the office of Master of the Horse as a reward for doing as she asked.

John White's illustration of The Arrival of the English in Virginia. *(Copyright The British Museum.)*

Philip Amadas was designated by Raleigh as admiral of Virginia and in April 1585 sailed on the *Roebuck*, Raleigh's 140-ton flyboat, with John Clarke as captain. Arthur Barlowe was most likely the captain of the *Dorothie*, Raleigh's pinnace or small bark, which may have turned back early as there was no mention of him or the ship during the voyage. Once again, Simon Ferdinando was along as master and chief pilot, sailing on the *Tiger*, the Queen's ship of 140–200 tons.

On board with Ferdinando was Sir Richard Grenville, admiral of the expedition and captain of the *Tiger*. In all there were 160 people on board, half of them crew members. Others of note on board were Thomas Hariot, assigned the scientific chores on the voyage; John White, the artist and surveyor; and Ralph Lane, appointed to govern. Also returning to Virginia were Wanchese and Manteo.

The second voyage to the Carolinas began on April 9, 1585, five days after the full moon, sailing the southern route to the Canaries. A storm off Portugal sank the small pinnace and scattered the fleet. Those remaining left the Canaries on April 14 for the West Indies, raising Dominica on May 7. Remaining for several days in the area they erected a fort for protection while they built a pinnace to replace the one that was lost, picked up cattle to take to Virginia, and finally departed on May 23, sailing around Hispaniola to Isabella. Grenville must have inspired his men with his famous energy in order to accomplish so much on Dominica in so little time.

Tiger, the flagship of the 1585 expedition to Roanoke Island. (Courtesy National Maritime Museum, London.)

On June 7 they sailed to a small island of the Turks and Caicos where they caught seals. Passing outside the Bahamas, they arrived off the land known as Florida and continued sailing north.

By June 25 the ships were foundering off the shoals of what Grenville thought was Cape Fear, but more likely they had arrived at Cape Faire (Cape Lookout). Entering through an inlet, they anchored at what one historian states was probably the harbor at Beaufort. Two days later they anchored off Woccocon—present-day Ocracoke—at latitude 35° north.

As they entered Pamlico Sound, *Tiger* ran aground but floated off at high tide. The rest of the fleet, including *Elizabeth*, a 50-ton bark with Thomas Cavendish as captain, hit bottom as well and was pounded over and over again by the sea. The crew managed to keep *Tiger* from completely wrecking, but the provisions and supplies were ruined.

On July 3 a message was sent to Wingina, the king of the Algonquian-speaking tribe at Roanoke Island, that the English were back. Meanwhile, the 100-ton ship *Lion of Chichester* with George Raymond as captain had landed three weeks earlier at Croatoan near Cape Hatteras and dropped off 30 colonists.

While most of the company were left anchored off the Outer Banks, Grenville, in his barge and with a pinnace and longboat carrying Lane, White, Hariot, Cavendish, Amadas, Manteo, and others, went in to explore the Pamlico Sound looking for a good site to settle the colony. Manteo was taken to his home on Croatoan Island, near Cape Haterask—known today as Hatteras Island. Wanchese had also returned with Grenville and saw many of the Caribbean islands before running aground on Woccocon in June 1585.

The men rowed and sailed 25 miles due north and landed. A few miles inland they found the Native American village of Pomeiooc and a great lake, Mattamuskeet. They continued their exploration, passing several bays, up the Pamlico River and its branch Pungo to the village of Aquascogoc. On July 15, after returning to the Pamlico Sound, they went another 20 miles to the village of Secotan where they were well entertained. It was at this time that White made sketches of the villages of Secotan and Pomeiooc.

An unfortunate incident over a silver cup apparently ruined the relationship they were building with the Native Americans, for the Europeans destroyed the village of Aquascogoc and returned to Woccocon, where they sailed north for six days, going 60 miles to Port Ferdinando on Haterask Island. Wingina's brother Granganimeo came on board and invited the explorers to visit at Roanoke Island, which they did based on Barlowe's report from the first voyage.

On August 5, John Arundel was sent to take a prize to England and to plead for relief and supplies. Three weeks later Grenville left on *Tiger*, leaving Lane in charge of the colonists, supplies, cattle, and plants that had not spoiled. He arrived in Plymouth on October 18, where he was met by a jubilant Raleigh and others. Meanwhile, on September 8, Lane had sent a message to England on the *Roebuck* complaining about Grenville and how awful he had been during the voyage and settling of the colony.

Life on Roanoke during the next months began peacefully enough. The remaining colonists built a fort designed by Hariot, with houses and garden areas, on the northern end of the island, and began their life in the new world. Although inept in native relations, even with Manteo as an interpreter, Lane still tried. He participated in a maize festival in August 1585 with more than 700 Native Americans in attendance. He learned how to grow corn and tried making syrup from the stalks. The winter was mild.

Roanoke was inaccessible to English privateers since inlets on the Outer Banks were too shallow for large vessels. Lane and others, realizing there was no deep water harbor, planned to go to the Hampton Roads area to see what it was like. In March 1586 they made their first attempt but only got to a native village near the headwaters of the Chowan River. On another trip they discovered Currituck Sound and rounded Cape Henry into Lynnhaven Bay. They also explored the Roanoke River to its headwaters.

But racial relations began to deteriorate. The Native Americans had received the first Europeans with joy, partly because they believed them to be men from heaven, since there were no women in their company and they refused the offer of native girls. Their hospitality seemed to indicate that the English could freeload forever, being supplied with food and whatever else they wanted because they were perceived as superior.

The Europeans did not understand the ways of the natives, who gorged in the fall when they had plenty and starved in the spring. They didn't gather and store as white men do. Wingina set up fish weirs and planted corn for the colonists in April, hoping it would see them through the summer. But the English didn't fish for themselves, they expected it from the natives. The English cattle and pigs, even though fenced in, would ravage the natives' cornfields. All of these differences and the unwillingness of the English to learn the native ways led to a Native American effort to remove the white man from their land.

Lane heard through Manteo that Wingina had gathered several hundred bowmen to do the job on the pretense of having a funeral for his father, who had always been able to control Wingina. Wingina also ordered that no food be supplied to the white man and he cut their fish nets so fish would escape. This caused a famine among the colonists. Also, the relief expedition with new supplies had not arrived. Lane sent Captain Edward Stafford, who commanded one of the pinnaces, and 20 men to live off Manteo's people at Croatan.

Lane's next move was to hold a preventative war and he planned a night attack on Wingina. On June 1, Lane and 25 of his men went to Wingina's mainland village and opened fire on Wingina and the others. Wingina played dead, but when he got up to run he was shot in the rear, chased into the woods, killed, and beheaded by two of the Englishmen, one of whom was Hariot. Lane prepared for a counterattack, but relief was nearby.

On June 8, 1586, Sir Francis Drake was returning from a raid in the West Indies, sailing near Croatan with his prizes. The lookouts sent word of Drake's approach to Lane and others, while Drake anchored offshore. He said he would

White's illustration of the Indian Village of Secotan. *(Copyright The British Museum.)*

leave a ship and some supplies for the colonists, but on June 13 a terrible nor'easter blew for four days and the ship that was to be left sailed for England instead. Drake offered to leave another ship, but by this time Lane and the remaining 103 survivors boarded Drake's ships and left Virginia. They arrived in Portsmouth on July 28.

Two days after they departed, a supply ship that Raleigh had sent arrived, looked for the colonists, and finding none, sailed home. By mid-July Grenville showed up with a fleet of ships and also looked for the colonists, but found that they had departed. He left 18 men to hold the fort, so to speak, for England and sailed on August 25, arriving in England in December.

A miniature of Sir Walter Raleigh by Nicholas Hilliard, c. 1584. (Courtesy National Portrait Gallery, London.)

THE THIRD VOYAGE: 1587

The third trip was to establish the "Citie of Raleigh" in the province of Virginia. In 1587, Raleigh named John White governor of the new colony. He was given a coat of arms by Raleigh and bought a suit of armor—for what reason no one seems to know—and sailed away on May 8 from Plymouth, England. His fleet was small considering he had with him 14 families including 89 men, 17 women, and 11 children. His daughter Eleanore, wife of Ananias Dare, and another woman were with child at the time.

Simon Ferdinando was again to be the fleet pilot, giving him carte blanche to privateer while at sea. The destination was Chesapeake, but when the fleet arrived on July 22 at Roanoke Island, it was discovered that the 18 men left by Lane the year before were gone. The fort had been razed, but the houses were still standing though overgrown with vines of melons and now housing local wildlife. Ferdinando, for his own reasons, made the decision that the colony would stay on Roanoke and not go to Chesapeake, so repairs were made and the colonists began to settle in. On August 13, Manteo was christened. Through June 1586 he had divided his time between his family home at Croatan and in guiding the English on trips through the local waterways.

Manteo returned to England with Lane in June 1586 and was an advisor to Governor White in preparation for the colony's establishment in 1587. In July of that year he accompanied Edward Stafford to Croatoan and when the remaining colonists left Roanoke in August, he stayed with them for their protection. It was for his loyalty and faithful service that he was christened by a command from Raleigh and given the title Lord of Dasamonquepeuc.

On August 18, 1587, White's granddaughter was born and on August 23 she was christened Virginia Dare. And soon after that Margery Harvey gave birth.

White concerned himself with making repairs to the broken friendship with the natives, visiting Croatoan Island with Manteo, where acting for Raleigh, he appointed Manteo chief of the Roanoke tribe. A month or so after arriving, White sailed for England. Upon his return, he met with Raleigh and planned for the reinforcement of the colony.

On April 22, 1588, White, along with 15 other civilians, sailed from Bideford, England but met up with two French ships that attacked them. They returned to England. Also in 1588, Thomas Hariot's report came out listing all the wonders of the new land but at the same time describing the deaths of the natives soon after they were visited by the white man.

During the span of more than two years, from fall 1587 to spring 1590, nothing is known specifically about what happened in North Carolina.

THE FINAL VOYAGE: 1590

It was on his eventual return to the colony that John White discovered the disappearance of the entire community. On March 20, White and a relief expedition sailed from England, spending time in the West Indies.

On August 3 they were offshore south of Cape Lookout, in foul weather. Staying at sea, they finally anchored August 9 at 35° 30' off the northeast corner of Croatoan. On August 15, the remaining two ships anchored off Cape Ferdinando, and the next day White and others rowed through the inlet to check on smoke they had seen on Hatteras Island. By August 17 they had landed at Roanoke and found no one. The only signs left were "CRO" carved in "faire Romane letters" on a tree on the brow of a forested sand dune. Going inland they found the ruins of the fort and houses. On a post at the entrance was "CROATOAN," carved in "fayre Capitall letters."

With no sign of a maltese cross that White had instructed be carved in the event of trouble, it appeared that the colonists may have decided to go to Manteo's island. White planned to go in search, but storms drove them away and back toward England. It is possible that during the intervening time the natives grew more restless, their crops failed, and the colonists saw no sign of relief.

It may never be known what happened to the Lost Colony. According to one historian, peaceful coexistence could have only happened if the Native Americans were willing to be slaves of the Europeans, but they were too proud for that and eventually lost their land because the Europeans could be resupplied by sea.

White's illustration of the Indian Village of Pomeiooc. *(Copyright The British Museum.)*

If Verrazzano and Raleigh, among others, had not been curious seekers of what is "over there," Virginia and North Carolina, as well as all of what we now know as the United States, might not have been discovered by Europeans until much later, and Beaufort's history would be much different. It appears that today's residents of Carteret County owe much to the early explorers and mapmakers, some of whom are discussed in greater detail in the following pages.

FERDINANDO, OR FERNANDES

Simon Ferdinando, or Fernandes as some historians write, was born on the Azore island of Terceira. He was trained in Portugal, then at the Spanish Casade Contratacion in Seville. He had made several voyages to the Orient, to South America, and up the North American coast, and was a successful pirate in the waters between the English Channel and the Azores, taking his prizes to England. He became a naturalized Portuguese pilot in the service of England, joined the Church of England, and was married in London. Ranked as a merchant and gentleman, he was called one of the best pilots in England by the Spanish high admiral.

In the 1570s, Ferdinando began an association with Sir Humphrey Gilbert, Sir Walter Raleigh's half-brother. In 1579–1580 he had reconnoitered the Penobscot estuary near Newfoundland to find a site for a colony. As a seasoned pilot with several voyages across the ocean prior to being chosen by Raleigh, one would think he would have been more careful when sailing along the Carolina coast. Some historians feel that either Ferdinando had lost some of his skills or he had been suborned by the Spanish secret service to wreck the expedition. It is possible, however, that he had never encountered such hazards as the shoals off the Carolina capes, and thus did not realize how dangerous they could be, even though he had studied the maps made by Verrazzano and others.

Ferdinando was the fleet pilot on all voyages for Raleigh. When Amadas and Barlowe were scouting in 1584, the inlet they discovered was named for Ferdinando. Port Ferdinando is believed by some historians to be Roanoke Inlet, which served the colony from 1660 to 1811, originally south of Nags Head. Others, however, believe it to be farther south, below the Cape Hatteras lighthouse where the Outer Banks are very narrow. For some reason, on the second voyage Ferdinando decided to anchor off Woccocon rather than continue north to his namesake inlet. His first mistake was made when he grounded *Tiger* upon entering this inlet. It was the beginning of the dislike of Grenville by both Ferdinando and Ralph Lane.

Appointed captain of the flagship for the third voyage, he crossed Governor White as well and couldn't have cared less for the colony. His primary interest was in privateering. He took it upon himself to sail wherever he wished and stop whenever it was convenient for him, not taking orders from anyone, even to the point of leaving the colony at Roanoke when it was to have gone to Chesapeake!

HAKLUYT

Richard Hakluyt was an interesting man. He was born in 1553 and educated at Westminster School and Christ Church in Oxford, where he received his master's degree and took holy orders. Although he continued to serve the church he also developed an interest in maritime history and geography, which most likely stemmed from a cousin of the same name who was a student of geographical studies.

Hakluyt was one of the earliest English collectors of data on previous voyages and maritime journals. His first book was titled *Divers Voyages Touching the Discoverie of America*, which became the basis for his larger work used by the planners of the Raleigh expedition. He wrote about the winds in the North Atlantic in the 1583 voyage of Gilbert.

In 1584, at the request of Raleigh, he wrote *A Discourse Concerning Westerne Planting*, which was given to Queen Elizabeth. She accepted the discourse, which was a plea for English settlement in America for many reasons, among them extension of reformed religion, supplying England with necessaries from her own dominions and not foreign countries, providing overseas bases to enlarge the queen's revenue, increasing the Royal Navy, and discovering a northwest passage. But Elizabeth ignored the advice for 30 years!

In 1584, Hakluyt was appointed chaplain to the English embassy in Paris, remaining there five years. He then went to Bristol Cathedral and was chosen by Raleigh as a member of his group of counselors, assistants, and adventurers. It was from his association with Raleigh and others that Hakluyt prepared his collection of *The Principal Navigations, Voyages, and Discoveries of the English Nation, made by Sea or Overland, Within the Compass of these 1500 Years.* His first volume was published in 1589, the third and last in 1600.

Sir Richard Grenville, captain-general of Raleigh's 1585 expedition to Roanoke Island. (Courtesy National Portrait Gallery, London.)

In 1605, Hakluyt was appointed to Westminster. His only ecclesiastical appointment was a rectory in Suffolk. He should have gone to Virginia in 1607 as rector of the church in Jamestown, but his age and infirmities prevented that. He was a diligent preacher, lived an exciting and irreproachable life, was married twice, and died in 1616 at age 64. He is buried in Westminster Abbey. If it had not been for Richard Hakluyt's insatiable desire for knowledge of sea voyages and exploration, and his desire to share this knowledge by translating and publishing these earlier adventures, the Raleigh expeditions would have had no clue what to expect when they arrived in North America.

HARIOT

Thomas Hariot was born in Oxford in 1560, received a degree in 1580, and was a mathematician. He was recommended to Raleigh to teach him the mathematical sciences. While at Raleigh's residence he taught navigation and astronomy to visiting sea captains. He may have been a member of the Amadas/Barlowe expedition in 1584.

For the second Raleigh voyage, Hariot was chosen as the expedition's scientist. Thus began a practice that lasted more than three centuries of adding scientific and artistic staff to expeditions.

Hariot was instructed to bring back detailed accounts of the physical characteristics of the flora and fauna of the places visited, to describe the people, and to make maps. To prepare for his study of the Native Americans, Hariot took Manteo and Wanchese into his care and taught them English while he learned Algonquian.

During his visit to the new world, he observed a variety of American conditions in the North Carolina sounds and his knowledge formed the textbook for future explorers. He wrote the commentaries that accompany de Bry's engravings of John White's paintings. He was an inveterate note-taker and more than 10,000 sheets of his notes survive in the British Museum in Sussex.

After Hariot's return to England he stayed with Raleigh, and in 1598 he went to Syon House, courtesy of the Ninth Earl of Northumberland. When Raleigh was imprisoned on a wrongful conviction in 1618 because of King James I and his relationship with the Spanish, Hariot visited often, taking books and assisting in laboratory experiments.

Hariot surpassed all contemporary mathematicians including his Oxford teachers and invented useful algebraic symbols. He improved optics, observed sun spots and moon spots with a 30-power telescope he built, and made the earliest known map of the moon. He invented an improved backstaff for determining latitude at sea and made a list of recommendations for the 1607 Jamestown expedition.

Hariot's *Brief and True Report of the New Found Land of Virginia* came out in February 1588. It was a catalogue of Virginia's native commodities including furs, deer skins, grapes, sassafras, silk grass (yucca), silkworms, alum, copperas, kaolin, cedar wood, pitch, tar, turpentine, and other naval stores derived from pine. He made much of the prospective copper mines and the beautiful pearls obtained by barter with the natives. He mentioned dye stuff from wood, pokeweed, sumac, and the native foods maize, kidney bean, pumpkins, squash, saltbush, and sunflower, describing how the natives planted and cooked them.

As a heavy smoker, Hariot mentioned uppowoc, or tobacco, as a cure-all for "grosse humors." He devoted several pages to edible roots, the groundnut, water plantain, arrow-arum, and wild onion. Fruits included chestnut, black walnut, acorn, shagbark, persimmon, prickly pear, wild strawberry, and scuppernong grapes used for wine.

He even listed "Beastes, Foule, Fishe" and building timbers. Above all, Hariot discussed the nature and manner of the Native Americans. Hariot died July 2, 1621 in London.

WHITE

John White was the artist who painted wonderful pictures and made accurate maps—for the day—during the second voyage to the Carolina coast and who, in 1587, was appointed by Raleigh as governor of the city of Raleigh in Virginia.

As a young man, White was a member of the Painters-Stainers Company of London and traveled with Martin Frobisher in 1577 on his second voyage. It was on this voyage that White painted the first European pictures of the Eskimo. Using watercolors, he was able to capture the detail of his subject. His painting of an Eskimo woman with her baby shows the hair on the sealskin and the needlework on her jacket.

Richard Hakluyt put John White's paintings in the hands of the Dutch engraver Theodor de Bry, whose illustrated works helped inform the European public about the English voyages of the time. White's illustrations were also used in Hariot's report of the new-found land of Virginia, which was translated by de Bry into Latin, French, and German.

It was also on this voyage that White depicted the fort at Mosquito Bay on St. John's Island in the West Indies, known today as Guayanilla Bay, Puerto Rico. His watercolor shows great activity. The detail included on the painting showed a blue heron, a ruddy duck, smaller birds, and land crabs. Everywhere he went White made sketches and watercolors. He even painted the scene at Cape Rojo when the crew was procuring salt.

According to one historian, White's record of the Carolina Algonquins is unparalleled in its accuracy. His drawings and paintings were made when he first met the tribes, who were at that time unaffected by European influences. White's drawings give detail of clothing, body decoration, and ornaments. White's map of Raleigh's Virginia from Cape Lookout north to the Chesapeake Bay is described as "the most carefully detailed piece of cartography for any part of North America to be made in the 16th century."

GRENVILLE

Sir Richard Grenville was a blue-eyed, brown-haired kinsman of Sir Walter Raleigh, a prominent figure from an old Cornish family, who was born in 1542. Grenville's father was also named Richard, and he was a poet and courtier under Henry VIII.

The younger Richard was elected to the House of Commons and married to Mary St. Leger, the daughter of a Devonshire Knight from Bideford North Devon. He fought the Turks in Hungary and the Irish in Ireland.

In 1571, Grenville returned to Parliament and was persuaded by Raleigh to go to Virginia, although he was not a professional seaman. He was hot tempered like Gilbert and Raleigh, and quarreled with Ferdinandes and Ralph Lane. But he also learned more ship handling than most sailors during his voyages to Virginia.

White's The Manner of Making Their Boats. *(Copyright The British Museum.)*

31

LANE

Ralph Lane was a young gentleman of means who owned shares in privateers. He fought in Ireland, but was greedy and confiscated the lands of the rebels. He was appointed equerry by the queen on his return to England and put in charge of 20 horsemen and forty foot soldiers kept at the palace. He was ready to undertake any command that her majesty might give.

While on the voyage to settle the colony, Lane was sent by Grenville in Puerto Rico to get salt from a captured Spanish ship. While the men were cutting chunks of salt from the cylindrical forms, a Spanish fleet arrived with a lieutenant in charge of 40 horsemen and 30 foot soldiers. But Lane exaggerated in his report stating that the governor of Puerto Rico was there as well. He complained to Grenville about being put in jeopardy, and thus began the quarrels that continued for the remainder of the voyage.

Lane stood up for Ferdinandes at every chance, which did not make for pleasantries on the ship with Grenville. When he wrote to Walsingham in England in September 1585, Lane said that Grenville had threatened to put him on trial for his life because he had offered unwanted advice! He begged to not be put under Grenville again for he could not stand his intolerable pride and ambition.

Thanks to Lane's explorations to the north, Raleigh planned his next colony to settle at Chesapeake where there would be deep-water access. In 1653, Francis Yeardley was shown the ruins of Lane's fort by the local Native Americans, and in 1709, John Lawson found old coins and guns at the fort site.

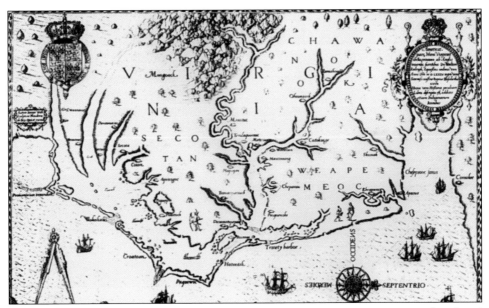

The 1590 White–De Bry map of the new world. (Courtesy NC Department of Cultural Resources, Division of Archives and History.)

3. Early Inhabitants

The Native Americans that were sketched and painted by John White lived near the coast and river estuaries near the outer banks. The coast there was warm, the waters were filled with fish and seafood of all kinds, there was plenty of game in the surrounding woods, and the soil was fertile.

The natives were very intelligent in their ways of farming, planting three crops in sequence and harvesting yearly in late September. To plant, the natives would clear and burn the area, build mounds of soil using digging sticks, then plant corn and beans together. During the fall and winter they gathered fruits, berries, nuts, and roots. They hunted game with bows and arrows and traps. They fished with spears and fish weirs, or nets. Clams, oysters, mussels, and other shellfish were also part of their diet.

Their two types of villages were described as open, such as Secotan, and enclosed, such as Pomeiooc. Houses were rectangular, made of bent and tied poles forming rounded roofs that were covered with matting or bark. Some were 36 feet by 72 feet. The occupants slept on benches around the walls, while open areas were kept for ceremonies and household activities. There may have been 100 to 200 people in a village.

Clothing was primarily of deerskin, with necklaces of pearl, copper, bone, and shells worn by both men and women. After their death, the dried bodies of chiefs were preserved in special houses with a religious image, cared for by a priest. Ceremonies were connected with their religion and with the seasonal cycle. Archaeologists have found beads, copper gorgets, feathers, and tattooing paint that was primarily used by the women, and body paint used by men and women.

The Algonquin

The Coree, Secotan, and Weapomeoc tribes were part of the Algonquin family, speaking a similar language (Algonquian) to other tribes found along the east coast from Cape Lookout to Maine.

Other Algonquian-speaking nations, such as the Shawnee, Miami, Illinois, Potawatomi, Kickapoo, Ojibwa/Chippewa, Menominee, Ottawa, Sauk, Fox, and Cree, were established in the Midwest and in Canada.

The name Algonquin, which means "fish spearers," came originally from a single village in Canada. However, the name spread and was ascribed to other smaller tribes along the coast of North Carolina. It was these Native Americans with whom the first English explorers had contact, and it was from them that the Europeans learned how to survive in the new world.

The Algonquin were more farmers and fishers than hunters. Their villages were usually near rivers or sounds that provided the fishing and good soil for planting. Their houses were built of saplings and bark. Each had a fireplace that was considered a holy place, as fire to the Algonquin was a gift from God. Food was also a gift of God and all food, plants, and animals had a living soul.

In the villages were sacred dance grounds, in the open air and marked by a ring of wooden posts carved with heads of ancestors and spirits. Many of the drawings of John White depict the Algonquin way of life, including his drawing of a medicine man known as the Flyer.

The medicine man was the go-between for people and spirits and had the capability of seeing into the future. These men healed the sick, forecast the weather, and consoled families at the time of death. It is interesting to note that when some of the slaves from Africa came to America they mixed with Algonquins. Out of this blend came the familiar Brer Rabbit stories. The Algonquin's spirit or great creator was pictured as a great rabbit or white hare, while the Africans' spirit was Anansi, a famous trickster.

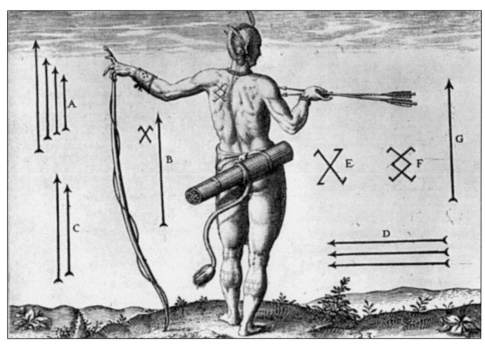

John White's 1585 illustration of The Marks of Sundry of the Chief Men of Virginia. *(Copyright The British Museum.)*

34

The Algonquin taught the early settlers about nature's power, but the white man gave them "evil" in return. Thus the chiefs organized large confederacies to resist the Europeans. The struggle ended on the east coast in 1675–1676 when the Algonquins were defeated, massacred, and driven from their land.

THE NATIVE CONNECTION

The east coast of present-day North Carolina was once the residence of several tribes of Native Americans, including Secotan, Weapomeoc, Coree or Coranine, and Tuscarora. The area now occupied by Beaufort and Carteret County was primarily the land of the Coree, and many of our sites still bear the name "Core," which presumably came from dropping the final "ee" sound from Coree.

Some examples of this are Core Creek, a canal connecting the Newport River with the Neuse; Core Banks, the easternmost outer bank that runs southwest to northeast from Cape Lookout to Portsmouth Village; Core Sound, the body of water between the mainland and the barren island known as Shackelford Banks, connected to the Pamptico, or as spelled today, Pamlico Sound.

The Newport River was originally the Coranine as indicated on Lawson's 1709 map. Legend has it that the change was made in the 1730s when the Bordens and Stantons came to Beaufort from Rhode Island and renamed the river in honor of their hometown.

The Hatteras Indians lived on the sand banks near Cape Lookout. Manteo's Croatoan Indians who offered refuge to Raleigh's colonists had survivors incorporated into this tribe. According to Lawson's history, published in 1701, several of the Hatteras Indians' ancestors were Europeans, and gray eyes were found among the natives. In 1700, the Hatteras Indians had one town, Sand Banks, with 16 fighting men and a population of about 80. During the Tuscarora War, they allied with the English.

In Carteret County, the Coranine, or Coree, lived in the area of Core Sound. Governor Archdale called them a bloody and barbarous people. Lawson listed them as Connamox with two towns, Coranine and Raruta, with 25 fighting men. By 1703, the Coree had become so abusive in their conduct that the government declared war on them. The Coree fought with the Tuscarora against the colonists. By 1715, when the Indian war was over, the Coree were allowed to settle at Mattamuskeet in Hyde County with the Machapunga Indians.

Lawson told of early warfare between the Coree and the Machapunga. In one instance the Coree invited the Machapunga to a feast after a peace was established between them following years of war. The Machapunga came with tomahawks hidden under their match, or blanket coats. Following the feasting and dancing, the Machapunga pulled out their tomahawks and killed several Coree, taking others prisoner. They later sold the prisoners to the English as slaves.

On Harkers Island in Core Sound, there was a shell mound marking a "feasting place of Indians." As this was Coree territory, this may have been where the feast took place between the Machapunga and Coree. The mound was nearly circular, about 100 yards in diameter, and 10 feet or more high in the center. There have been many excavations on the mound, and the shells were used to pave roads. The layers were well defined with an occasional fire pit showing. Clay pot pieces, pebbles, and animal bones were also discovered.

Lawson felt that the Carolina Indians were better to the white man than the white man was to the Indians. The native people always gave food freely at their quarters, yet the white people let them go hungry. The whites looked upon the natives with disdain and scorn and thought of them as "Little better than beasts in human form."

THE TUSCARORA WAR

The Tuscarora, of Iroquoian stock, were a fierce and aggressive tribe according to John Lederer and others in the 1670s. Their name means "hemp gatherers." The Tuscarora, as well as the Cherokee of the southern Appalachian mountains, were separated from their kinsmen to the north, the Five Nations. But the Neusiok, along the Neuse River, spoke the same language as the Tuscarora.

The Tuscarora lived along rivers inland. They also included tribes in the northeast such as the Conestoga, Mohawk, Oneida, Onondaga, Cayuga, Seneca, Huron, and Erie. They were hunters, farmers, fishers, and traders.

Lawson, in 1701, said the Tuscaroras had 15 towns and about 1,200 fighting men, with a total population of about 5,000. Their territory included the country drained by the Neuse River and its tributaries, the Contentnea and Trent Rivers, from near the coast to present-day Wake County, along the Tar-Pamlico River and perhaps the Roanoke. Their hunting area went as far as the Cape Fear River.

In 1710, emissaries of the Tuscarora appealed to the provincial government of Pennsylvania to let them move to a more friendly area where they would not be captured or killed by the growing numbers of settlers in the Carolinas. The answer to this request was delayed, and in the meantime a group of dissatisfied colonists led by Governor Cary incited the natives. Also, de Graffenried, who had brought settlers from Europe to the New Bern area, was treating the natives badly. Resentment grew among them. Adding to the tension was the "civil war" between Governors Cary and Hyde.

In September 1711, Lawson, who was surveyor general of the province, invited de Graffenried to go on a scouting trip up the Neuse River. They were captured by the Native Americans and taken to Catechna where the chief, King Hancock, called a council. Another council later that night included chiefs from other neighboring villages. Lawson and de Graffenried were questioned about their trip. After much debate it was decided to free Lawson and de Graffenried. But Core Tom, chief of Cartuka, was there and reproached Lawson for something. There was a quarrel, and Lawson and de Graffenried were condemned to death by a council of war. De Graffenried, however, was spared after speaking to the great assembly and giving them promises of a great reward for his freedom. An English-speaking Indian among them spoke to the others, and runners were sent to other Tuscarora villages, including that of the great chief Tom Blount, to invite the tribes to come watch the execution. On the return of the runners, de Graffenried was released, but Lawson was killed.

Lawson's execution was the beginning of the Tuscarora War. In addition to the Tuscarora under Chief Hancock were the Coree, Pamlico, Machapunga, or Mattamuskeet, Bear or Bay River, and others. Warriors went out to attack settlers along the Pamlico, the Neuse, and Trent Rivers and Core Sound as well as other nearby territories. There were 500 warriors in all. In the early hours of September 22, 1711, a war whoop signaled the onslaught. The massacre lasted three days, with death and destruction throughout the territory. The fortunate de Graffenried was kept at the encampment during this time, and heard of the massacre from one of the captured English. Two days later de Graffenried was turned loose.

An urgent appeal went out for help to quell the uprising. A detachment of soldiers from South Carolina under Colonel John Barnwell arrived in New Bern in January 1712, with 500 allied Native Americans who were enemies of the Tuscarora. The Tuscarora had an encampment called Fort Narhantes (Fort Barnwell) that was captured by Barnwell on January 30. The site was called Core Town by de Graffenried, indicating that the Coree Indians were prominent among the defenders of the fort. The next attack was at Catechna where Chief

White's Their Manner of Praying with Rattles about the Fire. *(Copyright The British Museum.)*

Hancock had his quarters. Twice they were repulsed, and a truce was entered into on condition the natives liberate the white prisoners. Barnwell returned to New Bern looking for honors, but there were none. He then assembled some friendly natives at Core Town and took them to South Carolina where they were sold into slavery. This caused the uprising to be renewed. Again the government in North Carolina called for aid from South Carolina. Colonel James Moore, with 33 militiamen and 900 Indians, joined the North Carolina force.

The Tuscarora to the north under Chief Tom Blount had not been involved in the uprising. The government sought their help too, but Colonel Moore's army arrived before any plan could be implemented. On March 20, they attacked Hancock's Catechna, and after three days the Tuscarora were defeated and the survivors fled north.

After the war, in 1715, the friendly Tuscarora and remnants of other tribes were united under Chief Tom Blount. A reservation was established along the Roanoke River, and more settlers began moving south into the Core Sound and North River area. In 1713, the town of Beaufort had been mapped, but in May 1714, the Coree Indians, being greatly distressed by the loss of lands and neighbors, began attacking white settlements in small skirmishes. The outbursts were finally ended in February 1715 with a treaty, and the Coree went to the territory of Mattamuskeet that was assigned to them. By the fall of that year, however, the attacks began again and conflicts continued sporadically until 1718. In 1802, the last chief of the Tuscarora in North Carolina, Samuel Smith, died. Following the Tuscarora War the settlement of Beaufort began in earnest.

White's Their Dances Which They Use at Their High Feasts. *(Copyright The British Museum.)*

4. THE SEVENTEENTH CENTURY

In the 1600s the Carolinas were still on the minds of the English, who were determined to colonize part of the new world and keep the French and Spanish from claiming it all. In 1603, Queen Elizabeth had died and King James I ascended to the throne of England. Sir Walter Raleigh was imprisoned on a wrongful conviction in 1618 because of James and his relationship with the Spanish. In 1630, Raleigh was released by the king but not pardoned. After an unsuccessful expedition to Guiana, James ordered Raleigh's execution to please the king of Spain. At age 65, Sir Walter Raleigh was beheaded.

The colony of Jamestown had been settled in 1609, and by 1653 their governor was Sir William Berkeley. As he had no authority in the area below the Chesapeake, many people moved there to escape his rule. Roger Green, a clergyman, led a colony to the banks of the Chowan and Roanoke Rivers.

In 1663, King Charles II, granted by charter on May 20 the same territory that had been conveyed to Sir Robert Heath in 1629. The grantees, with the consent of freemen, were to make laws, bestow titles of nobility, and authorize freedom of religion. Although none of the proprietors except Sir William Berkeley lived in the territory, they were all able to rule, sell land, and tax property. To provide for the transportation and expenses of colonists, the men formed a joint stock company.

This charter did not include the Albemarle region, so on June 30, 1665 a second grant was made extending the territory as far as the north end of the Currituck River or inlet, and on a straight line west to Weyanoke Creek, within about 36° 30' north latitude and west in a direct line as far as the south seas and southwest as far as 29° north latitude.

THE LORDS PROPRIETORS

Friends and relations of King Charles II were named lords proprietors of the Carolinas, the territory south of the lands not already granted to the province of Virginia to Spanish Florida. They included Edward Hyde, Earl of Clarendon; George Monck, Duke of Albemarle; William Lord Craven; John Lord Berkeley; Anthony Lord Ashley Cooper; Sir George Carteret; Sir William Berkeley; and Sir John Colleton.

Hyde was chosen because his daughter had married the king's brother. Monck had led the king's army, restored the monarchy and put Charles on the throne. The Earl of Craven had been a military officer who had advanced large sums of money to Charles. Cooper led parliament and was known as the Earl of Shaftsbury. Carteret was esteemed as the best seaman of the day and devoted fortunes to the Stuarts. Lord John Berkeley and Carteret became the owners of New Jersey in 1664. Sir William Berkeley was governor of Virginia and was the sole lord proprietor to actually live in the colonies.

Deaths of the proprietors changed the look of the rulers of the province. Sir John Colleton died in 1666 and his successor was Sir Peter Colleton. In 1669, George Monck died and his son Christopher, Duke of Albemarle succeeded him. Others took new offices, such as Sir George Carteret who became vice chamberlain to the king's household, and Sir John Berkeley who was appointed to the post of lord lieutenant of Ireland. His brother Sir William Berkeley was still the governor of Virginia.

On July 21, 1669, constitutions were adopted and signed by the lords proprietors to provide better settlement of government, establish interests of the proprietors equally, conform government agreeably to the monarchy, and avoid erecting numerous democracies in the province. Eight offices were established. One was the palatine, assigned to the oldest proprietor and transferred to the next oldest at his death. The palatine was the executive, while others were admiral, chamberlain, chancellor, constable, chief justice, high steward, and treasurer.

A map of the coast of Virginia by Mercator-Hondius.

Renaissance geographer Gerardus Mercator, left, and engraver/illustrator Jodocus Hondius. (Courtesy Library of Congress.)

At this time Carolina included what is now North and South Carolina and extended from the Atlantic to the Pacific Ocean. The land was divided into eight counties, one for each proprietor. Each county consisted of eight seignories, eight baronies, and four precincts, with each precinct divided into six colonies.

One seignory of 12,000 acres in each county was to be the property of a proprietor and would descend to his male heirs. A precinct of 72,000 acres contained land that could be bought and sold, but the purchaser had to pay the lords proprietors a yearly quit rent of a penny an acre.

A parliament would include the proprietors or their deputies, landgraves, caciques, and one freeholder from each precinct chosen by all freeholders, with each member having one vote. A freeholder was any white man having an estate of 50 acres. The parliament met on the first Monday of November every second year "in the town in which it last sat." Elections of freeholders were held on the first Monday in September every two years. On the first day of each January elections were held for an assemblyman.

Every county was to have a general court, held by the sheriff and one justice from each precinct. Each precinct had a court of a steward and four justices to judge all criminal cases except treason, murder, and other death penalty offenses, and criminal cases against nobility. A commission of itinerant judges would issue twice a year to try these cases. There were grand juries for criminal courts, and all verdicts were determined by a jury of 12 men, with the majority ruling.

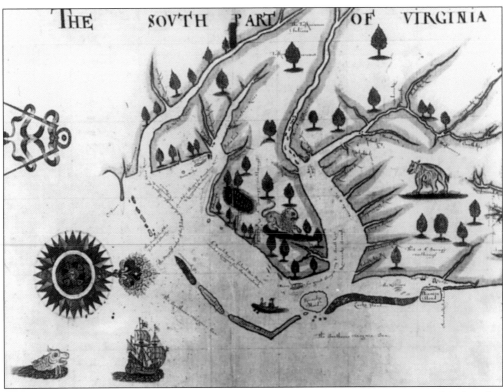

Comberford's 1657 map of the south part of Virginia. (Courtesy NC Department of Cultural Resources, Division of Archives and History.)

A register was to be in each precinct to record all deeds, judgments, and conveyances concerning land. In each seignory, barony, and colony a registry was to be available for recording births, marriages, and deaths.

Freedom of conscience was allowed. It took seven persons agreeing on any one religion to constitute a church or profession on which they should bestow some name to distinguish them from others.

Albemarle County was created first in 1663 and named for George Monck, Duke of Albemarle, with William Drummond appointed governor for a term of three years. Attention was called to the fact that Albemarle was not in the province of Carolina, that the limits of the province touched only the northern shore of the sound, and did not include plantations already there. The proprietors applied to the king for an extension of their grant 30 miles to the north. This was granted in 1665 and the Carolinas were extended to 36° 30' north, near the present boundary of Virginia and North Carolina, and also 2° farther south. The Cape Fear area was also settled at this time.

In 1667, trade was established between the Albemarle community, New England, and the West Indies. Corn, tobacco, and lumber were conducted abroad by New England vessels, while sugar, coffee and rum came into the province.

42

The government in 1668 included the governor, his council of 12 men, and 12 members of the House of Assembly elected by freeholders.

In 1670, Albemarle was divided into the precincts of Carteret, Berkeley, and Shaftsbury. Settlements quickly moved south along the coast eventually reaching Beaufort at Old Topsail Inlet. Four years later, the governor was dead and George Carteret succeeded him, resigning in 1676. By 1677, there were 2,000 taxpayers in the Albemarle area.

CARTERET CONNECTIONS

The lords proprietors most associated with Carteret County and Beaufort were Sir George Carteret and Henry Somerset. Sir George, born *c.* 1615, was known as Baron Carteret of Hawnes, the son of Helier de Carteret and Elizabeth Dumaresq, who married in 1608.

In 1649–1650, Prince Charles granted Sir George "a certain island and adjacent islets in America in perpetual inheritance, to be . . . held at an annual rent of £6 a year to the crown." This became the pattern Charles would follow with the rest of the proprietors.

Sir George died in 1680 and his grandson George Carteret, born in 1667, became Baron Carteret of Hawnes as well as inherited his share of the grant. His father, also named George, drowned in 1672, which accounts for the generation skip.

Grandson George served in the House of Lords, voting with the Whigs. He married Grace Grenville, the sister of John Grenville who had married Henry Somerset's mother. Grace was the daughter of John Grenville, first Earl of Bath who also was a lord proprietor, succeeded by his son John.

George died in 1695. His son John Carteret, born in 1690, inherited the Carolina share at his death. Carteret was educated at Westminster School and Christ Church, Oxford. In 1711 he took a seat in the House of Lords, a champion of the Protestant succession.

He was lord lieutenant of Devonshire from 1716 to 1721, and secretary of state during Walpole's administration, 1721–1724. From 1724 to 1730 John was lord lieutenant of Ireland.

John Carteret was also a favorite of George I and George II because he could speak German. In 1744, at the death of his mother, he became the Earl of Granville, and from 1751 to 1763 he was president of the council. He was unwilling to sell his proprietorship of Granville District to the crown in 1729.

John died in 1763 and Robert Carteret, born in 1721, inherited his father's title and share of the proprietorship. He was educated at St. John's College, Oxford, and by 1744 he was a member of parliament for Yarmouth on the Isle of Wight, serving for three years.

Robert Carteret held office on the Isle of Jersey from 1763 to 1776. His father disowned him when he married, and the title of Earl of Granville became extinct at his death.

BEAUFORT CONNECTIONS

The Beaufort name came from a prominent fifteenth-century English family descended from John of Gaunt (1340–1399) and his mistress Catherine Swynford. Through his eventual marriage to Swynford (his third wife), who died in 1403, Gaunt became an ancestor of the house of Tudor and a patron of Chaucer. Their three children, John of Beaufort, Earl of Somerset (died 1410); Henry Cardinal Beaufort, bishop of Winchester (1377–1447); and a third, were barred from succession to the throne, which was occupied by their cousins of the house of Lancaster from 1399 to 1461 (see appendix).

John of Gaunt was Duke of Lancaster, the fourth son of Edward III. By his first marriage to Blanche of Lancaster, who died in 1369, he became one of the most influential nobles in England. Their eldest son became Henry IV. John served under his brother Edward, the Black Prince in the 100 Years' War, and aided Peter the Cruel of Castile, married his daughter, and became king of Castile. As viceroy for his senile father Edward, he espoused his cause of court party and even ruled England for a time. From 1386 to 1388 he fought for claim to the throne of Castile against John I and also helped keep peace between Richard II and hostile barons.

John of Beaufort, Earl of Somerset was the father of two sons, John Beaufort, Duke of Somerset (died 1444); and Edmund Beaufort, Duke of Somerset

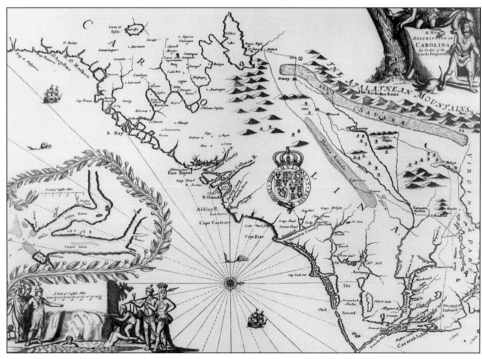

Ogilby's 1672 map of the coast of Carolina. (Courtesy NC Department of Cultural Resources, Division of Archives and History.)

A portrait of Sir John Carteret by an unknown artist.

(1407–1455). Edmund and his cousin Henry (1436–1464) were the leaders of the Lancastrian party during the War of the Roses. John's daughter was Margaret Beaufort (1443-1509) who married Edmund Tudor, Earl of Tudor, son of Catherine (who had been married to Henry V) and Owen Tudor. Margaret became Countess of Richmond and the mother of Henry VII, who became king after overthrowing Richard III in 1485. She founded Christ's College and St. John's College, Cambridge, and was a patron of Caxton.

Henry Cardinal Beaufort, bishop of Winchester from 1404 and cardinal from 1426, was an English prelate and statesman and the half-brother of Henry IV. He was chancellor from 1403 to 1404. After Prince Henry became Henry V, he again served as chancellor from 1413 to 1417. He swung English influence in 1417 to elect Pope Martin V. He was chancellor once more for Henry VI in 1424–1426 and a papal legate as well. He crowned Henry VI King of France in Parish in 1431.

The second Duke of Beaufort was Henry Somerset, born in 1684 to Rebecca Child Somerset and Charles Somerset, Marquis of Worcester. It was he for whom Beaufort was eventually named. His father, Charles, died in 1698 and his mother, Rebecca, married John Grenville, who, after a lengthy court action following the death of his kinsman the Second Earl of Albemarle in 1688, was declared the heir of the Monck estate. Henry succeeded to his grandfather's title of Duke of Beaufort, his grandfather having been an original lord proprietor.

Henry Somerset's stepfather John Grenville was the brother of Grace Grenville who married George Carteret. Carteret had no children, so the share went to Henry's mother who transferred it to Henry. In 1705 Henry had a seat in the House of Lords. He was lord lieutenant of Hampshire, Gloucestershire, and other cities of Bristol and Gloucester. In 1712, he was made a Knight of the Garter.

Henry was married twice. With his second wife, Rachel, he had three sons, two of whom succeeded to titles and property. Henry died in 1714 and his share was inherited jointly by Henry Somerset, born 1707, the Third Duke of Beaufort, and his brother Charles Noel Somerset, born 1709, the Fourth Duke of Beaufort.

The Third Duke of Beaufort took his seat in the House of Lords in 1728 and in 1729 was elected high steward of the city of Hereford. He was married but had no children and died in 1745. His brother Charles Noel succeeded to the title of Fourth Duke of Beaufort when Henry died. Charles was 20 when his share of the proprietorship was sold to the crown. He became a member of parliament for Monmouth and served in the House of Lords. He was married, had one son and five daughters, and died in 1756.

Benjamin West's 1779 portrait of George III. (Copyright Her Majesty Queen Elizabeth II.)

5. THE EIGHTEENTH CENTURY

The seventeenth century ended with a severe fever that ran rampant through the area of Pamlico and Core Sounds in 1696, destroying nearly all the Native American tribes and appearing to make it safe for southern exploration. In addition, the price of land and the annual quit rents in the area south of the Albemarle were much less than in the more developed part of the colony. Settlements began springing up along the Neuse River to the north of today's Carteret County at the dawn of the eighteenth century.

LAWSON

According to one historian who edited and republished the history of North Carolina, Lawson was most likely the son of Andrew Lawson of London, and served an apprenticeship as an apothecary.

Educated and trained in the natural sciences, Lawson was preparing to travel to Italy when he ran into a young man who convinced him that seeing the American continent would be more exciting and fruitful. Thus, Lawson left the Thames around May 1, 1700. Three months later he arrived in New York harbor. After a two-week stay, he gathered his supplies and sailed to Charleston, South Carolina around the end of August.

In December of that year, Lawson was appointed by the lords proprietors to make a reconnaissance survey of the interior of the Carolinas. By February 12, 1701, Lawson and his traveling companions reached the town of Occaneechi, near present-day Hillsborough. He met Enoe Will, a Native American guide who agreed to lead him to the English-speaking settlements on the coast. They traveled along the western bank of the Neuse and crossed over at the "falls" to the northern bank on February 18.

The Neuse River, for those who are unfamiliar with it, runs from the area around Durham southeast to the Pamlico Sound. Thus Lawson and his group were following this course until they passed the site of Goldsboro. They then turned north and crossed over the Contentnea Creek and then the Tar River near Greenville. From there they continued to an English settlement near the "original" Washington on the Pampticough River where they arrived February 23.

In 59 days during the winter months, Lawson and his fellow travelers had covered approximately 550 miles. During the entire exploration Lawson kept a journal, taking copious notes on everything he saw, tasted, and smelled, as well as beginning a language book of various Indian words.

During the spring of 1701 Lawson moved from the Pamlico area south to a fork in the Neuse River and built a house about a half mile from a native town. There he lived with a young Native American and a bulldog. The native town was to become known as New Bern, and the creek on which Lawson built his house was named for him.

It is apparent that Lawson was engaged in surveying. On April 28, 1708 he was appointed by the lords proprietors as the successor to Edward Moseley, the former surveyor-general of the colony, and in 1709 he surveyed the area north and east of the Cape Fear River.

During Lawson's residency in North Carolina there were issues with religious freedom, establishment of the Church of England, and discrimination against Quakers and other dissenters who were living in the colony. In 1710, this all came to a head with the Cary Rebellion. Thomas Cary, the self-proclaimed governor of the colony, was really only the president of the council who happened to serve in that capacity for three years from 1708 to 1711.

Thomas Pollock, one of the largest land owners and a powerful political figure and close friend of Lawson, along with the lords proprietors, did not recognize Cary as governor. The rebellion came to an end in 1711 when Cary left for Virginia. Edward Hyde was then appointed the first true governor of North Carolina. It was, however, during these three years of turmoil that the Tuscarora decided the time was right to attack the white people who had settled their land.

The settling of the North Carolina–Virginia line came about while Lawson was the surveyor-general of the colony. In 1699, a royal order to survey the line was ignored in Virginia, although in 1665 the land in controversy had been granted to Carolina with the move of the northern line. In 1709, Queen Anne ordered the two colonies to adjust the boundary. Lawson, although in England at the time looking into publishing his book, was appointed with Edward Moseley as commissioner on the part of Carolina to survey the lands in dispute. However, the dispute was not settled until 1728.

Lawson was involved in the incorporation of Bath on March 8, 1705. He bought property, made a home, and was active in the politics and economics of the town and county. He served as clerk of the court and public register of Pampticough Precinct from 1706 to 1708.

Following his move south, Lawson also helped establish the town of New Bern. Baron Christoph von Graffenried had purchased from the lords proprietors more than 17,000 acres located at the juncture of the Neuse and Trent Rivers. Lawson sold part of his property as well and was instrumental in helping von Graffenried bring his Swiss colonists to settle the area in 1710.

Von Graffenried then authorized Lawson to lay out the lots of the town, based upon his plan.

John Lawson's map of the Carolinas from the 1709 edition of A New Voyage to Carolina. *(Courtesy North Carolina Collection, University of North Carolina [UNC] at Chapel Hill.)*

When the Tuscarora attacked the settlements in 1711, Lawson was one of the first victims. His will, written in 1708, left to "his dearly beloved" Hannah Smith the house and lot in which he was living and one-third of his personal estate. The remainder was to be divided between his daughter Isabella of Bath Town and her unborn brother or sister.

We are fortunate indeed to have Lawson's journal *A New Voyage to Carolina* reprinted for our generation and future generations of researchers to read and learn from. He describes the North Carolina of the time in great detail, such as this description of Beaufort's harbor: "Topsail Inlet is above two Leagues to the Westward of Cape Look-out. You have a fair Channel over the Bar, and two Fathom thereon, and a good Harbour in five or six Fathom to come to an Anchor. Your Course over this Bar is almost N.W. Lat. 34° 44"."

SAFE HARBOR

Nearly 300 years ago, when Queen Anne was on the throne of England and the lords proprietors were in charge of exploration and settlement in the new world, Beaufort became a town inhabited by settlers from the northeastern area of the Carolina Territory seeking a natural, deep-water port with easy access to the ocean.

Early owners of Beaufort believed that Core Sound and Cape Lookout bight should become a major Atlantic coast seaport. The harbors in the county were well protected by the outer banks, and yet they were near the open sea. Early settlers found the sounds, rivers, and creeks teeming with seafood. There were excellent stands of timber with longleaf pine that could supply a source of tar, pitch, and turpentine. The forest provided wild game for food and furs. The soil was rich, the climate moderate, and there was an ample supply of fresh water.

Lack of transportation to the inland areas, however, made growth in Beaufort and Carteret County difficult. In colonial days, the means of transportation was primarily by water. New Bern, near the head of the Neuse River, had direct water access to the Pamlico Sound and through Ocracoke Inlet to the Atlantic Ocean. Edenton, on the Albemarle Sound and near the Chowan River, also had access to the Atlantic through the inlets along the northern outer banks. The Cape Fear area had direct connection to the Atlantic. This made New Bern, Edenton, and the Cape Fear area important ports, for not only did they all have access to the open ocean, they were all on rivers leading to the interior of the province.

In Carteret County the harbors were used primarily to ship only those products produced in the county and to import those items necessary to the local residents. In storms they served as refuges for ships traveling north and south. This problem was defined by Governor Arthur Dobbs at a board of trade meeting in London. As he stated, Topsail Inlet had a safe harbor with deep water and no bar, but no navigable river leading to it.

Several notations make it clear that the Core Sound area was being slowly settled. On von Graffenried's map of 1710 is a notation describing Core Sound being populated by English who supplied seafood of all kinds to settlers inland. There was also a sloop plying the waters named *Core Sound Merchant*, owned by Captain Edward Allard. A third indication of settlement was the order of March 12, 1712 by the general assembly that a fort should be built on Core Sound with a garrison of 30 men to guard settlers in the area from the Coree Indians.

In Maurice Davis's book about the Hammock House, there is a wonderful description of the surroundings of Beaufort. Old Topsail Inlet, he states, "offered a relatively safe haven from the frequent coastal storms off the Carolina Capes." Pirates used the sound and Cape Lookout bight to restock their ships with water and meat, and possibly to trade with the local Coree Indians. Harkers Island is but a short distance from the cape, near Beaufort, and early in the 1700s fishermen were asking for protection from the government.

BEAUFORT IS BORN

Although Lawson never settled in the area of Core Sound and the Core River, his description gives us some idea of why the area was important to the lords proprietors and the persons in charge of the colony. It was around 1709 when the town located on the site of the former Coree Indian village, Cwarioc, meaning "fish town," was established.

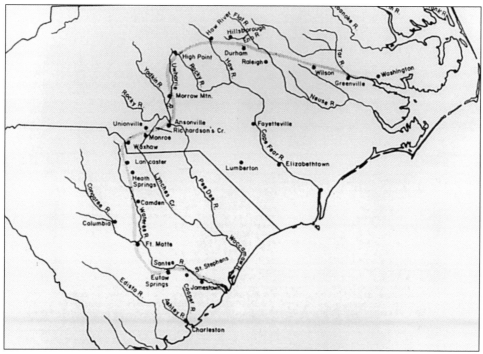

A map of Lawson's Long Trail. (Courtesy North Carolina Collection, UNC at Chapel Hill.)

Early owners of the small town at the west end of the land surrounded by the Core Sound, known today as Taylor's Creek and the Newport River, included Farnival Green (1707–1713), Robert Turner (1713–1720), Richard Rustull (1720–1725), and Nathaniel Taylor (1725–1733).

Following the end of the Tuscarora War in March 1713, Farnival Green, on July 18, assigned his earlier patent to Robert Turner, a merchant from Craven County, who had Richard Graves, the deputy surveyor, lay out the town that was to be called Beaufort.

A map was drawn and streets were named. Anne and Queen Streets were named for the queen. Moore Street was named after the colonel who had come from South Carolina to end the war. Orange Street was named for William the Third who had occupied the throne prior to Queen Anne. The only road into town was called Turner Street after Robert Turner, the new owner of the town. Pollock Street was named for Thomas Pollock, who was governor, and Craven Street was named for William Lord Craven, one of the lords proprietors. There was no street along the water until the 1800s; it eventually became known as Front Street.

On April 4, 1722, Beaufort was appointed a port for the unloading and discharging of vessels by the lords proprietors' deputies. The first commissioners of the town were Christopher Gale, John Nelson, Joseph Bell, Richard Bell, and Richard Rustull.

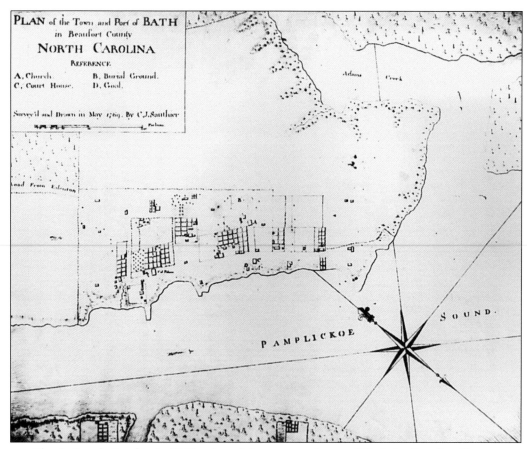

Claude Joseph Sauthier's 1770s plan of the town and port of Bath in Beaufort County. (Courtesy State Department of Archives and History.)

Incorporation took place on November 23, 1723, and five lots were sold, all of which lapsed for non-payment or for not having a building erected on them. The law stated that when a person purchased a lot, a house or building of at least 15 feet by 20 feet must be built within two years or the property would revert back to the town or the previous owner.

Five years later in 1728, a new section of town was added and deeds began distinguishing Old Town from New Town. Pollock Street was the dividing point, thus everything west of Pollock to Gallants Channel was Old Town while New Town went from Pollock east to Gordon Street.

Each section had lots along the waterfront that measured 66 feet across and 330 feet deep. The remaining lots in both sections were set aside as 110 feet on the street side and 198 feet running east and west. The only exception to this was in the block bounded by Moore, Broad, Orange, and Cedar Streets where the lots were the entire width of the block east and west (396 feet) and only 55 feet wide on Moore and Orange Streets.

Between 1728 and 1732 deeds were recorded for 21 new lots, 16 of which were lapsed and 5 of which transferred ownership. In 1728, the governor commented that Beaufort had "but little success and scarce any inhabitants." Nine years later John Brickell, in his *Natural History of North Carolina*, described Beaufort as "small and thinly inhabited." In 1748, there were only 320 taxables listed for the county.

Charles Paul states in a 1963 paper that one of the most vivid accounts of Beaufort was given by a French traveler who visited the town 200 years earlier. He described it as a "small village not above 12 houses, the inhabitants seem miserable, they are very lazy and indolent, they live mostly on fish and oisters, which they have in great plenty."

Between 1765 and 1770, 37 lots changed hands and 9 had substantial buildings on them, primarily at the west end of Front Street. This is apparent from Claude Joseph Sauthier's map from the 1770s, which shows houses mostly along the waterfront with a few other buildings spread throughout the village. The majority of the houses built at this period are still standing today, with many featured on the Historical Association's annual Old Homes Tour.

FORMATION OF CARTERET PRECINCT

In January 1722, a petition was sent from the inhabitants of Core Sound showing that the lords proprietors had appointed Core Sound a free port and that several people had settled there and more were expected. The precinct courts were kept at the Neuse and it was a hardship to travel there to attend court, so the inhabitants requested that a new precinct be erected independent of the Neuse and that a commission be granted them with the same privileges as other precincts.

In August of the same year, the council met at the home of Thomas Pollock, president, with Christopher Gale, John Lovick, and Thomas Pollock Jr., the lords proprietors' deputies, present. It was resolved that according to the former order of the council to make Core Sound a separate precinct, the new precinct should be called Carteret. Thus it was in 1722 that Carteret Precinct was formed from Craven Precinct, Bath County.

The bounds would include all lands lying on Bogue Sound and the rivers and creeks running into them including all the settlements south of them, until further division of other counties or precincts. Craven was to consist of the settlements on the Neuse and Trent Rivers and their branches including Bear River. Justices of the peace appointed to govern the new territory included John Nelson, Richard Rustull, Enoch Ward, Joseph Bell, and Richard Whitehurst.

THE CHURCH OF ENGLAND

The Church of England began in the colonies with the founding of the first permanent settlement in Virginia. The first missionary sent to the Carolina Province was the Reverend John Blair who arrived in 1704, stayed several months, then returned to England due to poverty and sickness. Blair wrote about his experiences and described the hardships that would confront any other prospective Anglican missionary. Swamps, unbridged rivers, the high cost of horses, inadequate financial support, the apathy of most inhabitants and hostility of some, the lack of churches, chapels, and libraries, all were included.

Blair's assessment of the religious affiliation of the population was divided into four sorts of people: Quakers, whom he saw as the most powerful enemies of the church government; Presbyterians of a sort who preached and baptized throughout the country with no order from any church or sect; a great many with no religion; and those who were zealous for the interest of the church, who he admitted were few in number.

In 1709, there were four precincts or parishes in the Albemarle region: Chowan, Pasquotank, Perquimans, and Currituck. There were three in the Pamlico region: Beaufort, Hyde, and Craven. In Chowan Precinct was St. Paul's Parish in Edenton, established in 1701. This parish was divided in 1715 and Southwest Parish was established. In 1722, the parish was again divided and South Shore Parish was created, becoming known as St. Andrew's Parish in 1729.

Bertie County was divided from Chowan in 1722, and Society Parish was established at the same time. In 1727, Society Parish was divided to form North West Parish, and in 1729, Tyrell County was formed from Chowan, Bertie, Currituck, and Pasquotank Counties. St. Andrew's Parish was established at the same time.

Craven Parish was established in 1715 and in 1741 it became Christ Church Parish. St. Thomas Parish was established in 1701 in Beaufort Precinct. St. Thomas Church is the oldest original church building in North Carolina, having been erected in 1734. In 1722, Bath County was divided, creating Carteret Precinct. St. John's Parish was most likely established at the same time, and is mentioned as early as 1724.

St. John's Parish, of Carteret Precinct and Beaufort, existed through the Revolution with the vestrymen changing their titles to wardens of the poor and continuing to meet yearly until 1843. The original vestry minutes of St. John's Parish were rescued in the 1900s when the fourth courthouse was being dismantled and records were being tossed.

The vestrymen of St. John's Parish in 1723 included Christopher Gale, Joseph Bell, Jno [John] Shaw, Jno Nelson, Richard Whitehurst, Richard Williamson, Richard Rustull, Jno Shackelford, Thomas Merriday, Enoch Ward, Joseph Fulford, and Charles Cogdell. Prior to this date, apparently, William Davis and sons and Joseph Wicker were serving.

It is interesting to note that the first commissioners of the town of Beaufort included Christopher Gale, John Nelson, Joseph Bell, Richard Bell, and Richard Rustull. And in 1727, the first justices of the court were John Nelson, Richard Rustull, Joseph Bell, Richard Whitehurst, Ross Bell, Joseph Wicker, Enoch Ward, and Charles Cogdell.

Another interesting fact is that several of the vestrymen serving in Beaufort were also vestrymen in other parishes. Christopher Gale was also at St. Thomas,

*Sauthier's plan
of the town of
Newbern in
Craven County.*

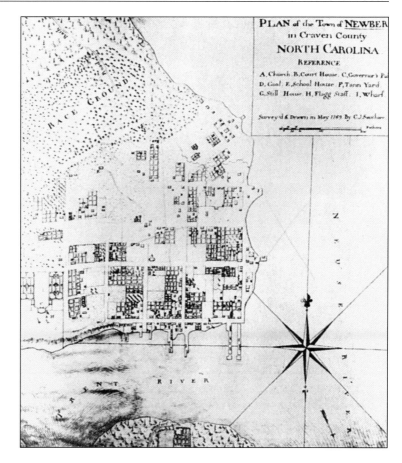

Bath; and Joseph Bell and John Nelson served in Craven Parish, New Bern. John
Bell, although not a vestryman at St. John's Parish, Beaufort, was with St. Peter's
Parish in Pasquotank. Joseph Wicker was also with Currituck Parish. There were
also several members of other parishes who were involved in the beginnings of
the town of Beaufort.

By 1728, Joseph Wicker was the warden and it was he who ordered William
Davis to be paid for rebuilding the church/courthouse that had been destroyed
by fire and storm. In 1739, Joseph Bell was a warden, and by 1742, when the
surviving records begin, the vestrymen were Thomas Lovick, James Winwright,
Arthur Mabson, John Shackelford, Edward and Enoch Ward, David Shepard,
George Read, Charles Cogdell, W. Lovick, Daniel Rees, John Frazier, Thomas
Austin, and Joseph Bell.

The vestry met periodically during the year, primarily to levy taxes or settle
accounts of former wardens. The main meeting of the vestry was usually on the
Monday following Easter. It was then that new wardens were chosen, readers of
divine service were appointed, taxes were levied, and other cares of the parish
were discussed and solutions decided.

Services were held every other Sunday at first in the Beaufort church building. As more and more people settled in the area the services were expanded to chapels built in the most populated parts, with lay persons appointed to read divine service. It was, however, only four times a year that a priest from Christ Church Parish in New Bern would come to St. John's Parish and hold Eucharist.

Research completed within the past three years indicates that the previously unidentified lot used by the Church of England in Beaufort was most likely Old Town 101, on which sits Purvis Chapel AME Zion Church today. Under the present church building are piers, or pillars, that most likely supported the original building, which was burned and blown away in 1725.

The Church of England was not the only religious organization in the area in the 1700s. The Quakers had settled in the Core Sound area and built their Core Sound Meeting House. Many of the early settlers who helped build the area,

An early local windmill. (Courtesy Beaufort Historical Association.)

and were Quakers, included the Bordens and Stantons who were ship builders and farmers, and Robert Williams who arrived later in the century and was very active in the community as an owner of a variety of parcels of land. Although not specifically in Beaufort and Carteret County, Presbyterians and Baptists were among settlers across the state.

By the latter part of the century, especially following the Revolution, the Methodists had moved into the area and prospered. Whitefield had passed through in 1739 and again in 1764, and although he regarded himself as a member of the Church of England, he was an advocate of the Methodist way. He preached in New Bern while traveling in the country. Religion, no matter what sect, was an important part of the life of the people of the town and the county.

THE COURTS

It was a heavy, tiresome, and sometimes frustrating job being a justice in the court during the eighteenth century. The court met quarterly, but sometimes the weather was terrible, with ice and snow or hurricanes that made traveling to and from the court very treacherous. There were not many bridges at the time, so if a justice lived on the "other side of the river" from Beaufort, they would have to either cross on a ferry, find a smaller stream and ford it, or just go around. Sometimes they met very early in the morning or adjourned to later in the evening, depending on the heat of the day.

The original courthouse was a building that was already in place when the court was established. By 1728, a new building was erected to replace the first, which had been destroyed by fire and hurricane. As with most buildings in the eighteenth century, there were no windows as we know them today. In fact, the truth is that a window is merely an opening in a wall. What we have today are the sashes and window panes that go into the window that only began to be installed in the county in the 1800s.

So it was that the gentlemen of the community who were chosen as justices and vestrymen had to meet in a small one-room building with no sash or glass in their windows, in the cold of winter when there was no heat, and in the heat of the summer with all the bugs. It is possible that then, as now, the spring and fall meetings were not terribly bad. But it must have taken a lot of fortitude and desire for these persons to serve so faithfully in both church and court.

The early court minutes of Carteret Precinct began in June of 1724. The Honorable George Burrington commissioned the following as justices for the Carteret Court: John Nelson, Richard Rustull, Enoch Ward, Richard Whitehurst, Joseph Bell, and Joseph Wicker.

In December, court was held for the Port of Carteret with Captain John Nelson, Richard Rustull, Richard Whitehurst, Captain Enoch Ward, and Joseph Wicker present. And thus it continued throughout the 1700s. Each of the court minutes was begun with the listing of those present. If there were not enough, court would be adjourned until they could find enough of the justices to participate.

The clerk of court for Carteret Precinct in 1724–1725 was Joseph Wicker. From 1727 to 1729, John Galland (or Gallant as the channel named for him is called today) served as clerk. At one session, he was ordered by the justices to find them dinner on the first day of court and was told he would be reimbursed for his trouble. John Simpson was clerk from 1729 to 1730, when the job went to James Winwright. In 1741, George Read became clerk and served until 1755, when Jacob Shepard served as deputy clerk. For a few years others in the community served as clerk, until Robert Read was chosen. He continued well into the 1770s.

Jurists were selected at each prior court session, naming several men from whom a jury of 12 could be chosen. Serving on a jury was to be an honor and a privilege, although sometimes the selected persons were not able to get to court due to weather or some other circumstance. The jurors were paid for their trouble, particularly when they had to travel to New Bern to attend the district court. Sometimes a jury was selected to lay out a road in the community, sometimes to settle a dispute, other times it might be for laying out the bounds of one's property, but their primary job grew into what juries do today.

Constables, marshals, and sheriffs were a big part of the court. They served in a variety of ways, not only in the courtroom during a session, but also taking lists of tithables for the taxation, making sure their particular area was kept safe, and escorting interlopers from Carteret back to the county from whence they came. Inspectors were also appointed and each of those appointed were instructed to enter into bond of surety with the court.

Besides the courthouse there was the matter of incarceration. The first jail in town was built by Daniel Rees on lot 7 in Old Town, which is where Queen Street is today. The location was at the water front, next to William Thomson's lot and wharf. The design of the building was very precise. The length was to be 20 feet, with a 15-foot width. Walls were to be sawed logs not less than 4 inches thick and dovetailed at the corners. Floors above and below were to be laid with plank not less than 4 inches thick.

A partition was to be in the middle of the prison with a door and lock, as well as one strong double door on the outside not less than 3 inches thick with good strong hinges and a substantial lock. Two front windows, 2 feet high and 18 inches wide with proper iron grates were provided for. The roof was to be covered with good pine shingles well nailed. The jail was to be completed in four months from December 10, 1736, and Rees was to be paid for his performance and work at £135.

Commissioners James Salter, Thomas Dudley, and Captain Ward were appointed to see that the work was done. Into the bargain, Rees was to make a substantial pair of stocks.

To pay for the building of the jail, a poll tax of 5 shillings was levied against every tithable in the precinct. The marshal was to be paid 10 shillings of the money collected for his services. A year later, the court ordered the marshal to collect and levy another 7 shillings 6 pence from each tithable in the precinct to help pay the charges for the building.

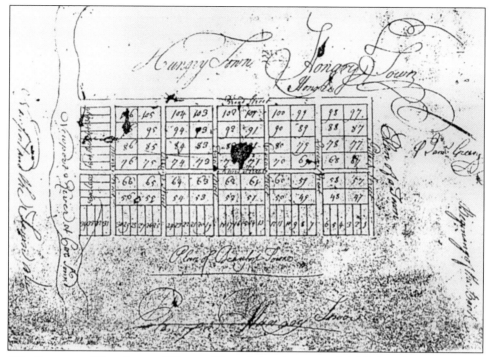

The first map of Beaufort, or "Hungry Town," showing original Old Town lots.

By 1743 the jail needed repairing, as did the courthouse. The funds for this were to be paid from the public money of the county. The court appointed Colonel Thomas Lovick and Captain Arthur Mabson to find the proper workmen to do the repairs. The vestry of St. John's Parish also ordered the church wardens to "cause the court house and prison to be put in good repair."

Over the years, both buildings were in need of repairs or entire rebuilding. By 1796, a third courthouse was built in the middle of the crossing streets of Ann and Turner. It stood there until 1837 when it was moved to the northeast corner, and a new courthouse was built on Courthouse Square. Today, the 1796 courthouse is on the restoration grounds of the Historical Association and has been totally restored to its original splendor.

Road overseers were appointed by the court to make sure that whatever roads there were were kept in good order, repaired, rebuilt, or moved as necessary. They were also in charge of the people in their district that were to do the work. Other appointments by the court included commissions to find a good site and have a fort built, hear persons who wished to build a mill on their property, and serve as the go-between with the neighbors.

The court issued deeds to the properties that were bought, sold, or exchanged. There were attorneys who served for various people who may not be available when needed, or were sick and could not come to court. Wills and estates were registered and settled in the court. Orphans were apprenticed or turned over to a guardian or

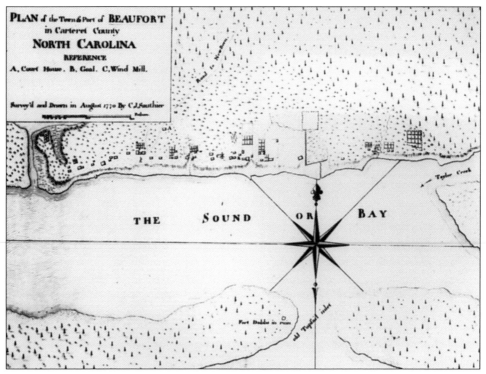

Sauthier's plan of the town and port of Beaufort. (Courtesy NC Department of Cultural Resources, Division of Archives and History.)

indentured. The court dealt with the slave and Native American issues that arose during the year. They issued licenses for public houses and ordinaries as well as liquor licenses. They set the cost of "victuals and drink" that were served in the taverns or ordinaries.

PIRATES!

In the late 1600s the ruse of tying a lantern about a horse's neck and walking along the shore with it was used to lure ships at sea onto the banks, where they could be scuttled and robbed. Presumably the victims believed the lanterns were the stern lights of another ship, which they would follow for safety. The name Nags Head, from the horses or "nags," is supposed to have derived from just such a practice.

Pirates had been roaming the Atlantic coast for years with bases in the Bahamas. Edward Teach, better known as Blackbeard, was one of the more infamous. Stede Bonnett, a gentleman by birth and well educated, was one of Blackbeard's lieutenants and they had friends everywhere in Virginia and in North and South Carolina. Occasionally pirates would come into the Pamlico Sound to visit and resupply. Some people were indignant that these pirates were allowed to roam so freely and were tolerated by government officials.

Although quite unbecoming in looks with his long black braided hair, Teach apparently could be extremely charming and yet excessively brutal. Along with others who took advantage of the inlet and bight of Cape Lookout, he periodically used the area, including the Beaufort harbor, as a place of rest, rejuvenation, and refilling of supplies for his ship.

It is said that Blackbeard was a frequent visitor to Core Sound, perhaps residing at the Hammock House when in the neighborhood. He would, according to legend, merely anchor his ship in the creek, row to the house, and tie up on the porch post. There are other stories about his association with the Hammock House as well, including the burial of treasure in the yard, although none has been found.

After 1718, when Blackbeard and others had been driven away from the Bahamas by the English, he began making his headquarters near Bath. Records say that Blackbeard and Bonnett visited the Core Sound area in 1718 and commented that Beaufort was a "poor little village at the upper end of the harbor."

In June, when Blackbeard put his and Bonnett's ships into the Old Topsail Inlet, he tricked Bonnett into going on to Bath. Blackbeard then sank both ships, leaving the crews to fend for themselves. He took off in the only ship left and carried his booty away. It is possible that some of the stranded seamen settled in the area rather than take a chance on being hanged as pirates. According to Maurice Davis, one was said to have made his way back to New England, but later returned to Carteret Precinct and became a man of some importance.

When the king offered a pardon for any pirate who would turn himself in and turn his life around, Blackbeard took advantage of the offer, but his new life only lasted about a month before he was back on the high seas. One excursion brought a cargo of oranges and other fruit, with sugar and spices that he had removed from a French vessel captured in August near Bermuda and later burned along the Carolina coast. Apparently, Blackbeard stored some of his booty in a barn belonging to Tobias Knight, the secretary of the colony as well as chief justice while Christopher Gale was absent.

The governor of Virginia, determined to capture and rid the ocean of pirates, sent two sloops into North Carolina waters where they discovered Blackbeard's ship the *Adventure* near Ocracoke. Following an intense battle, the British crew managed to kill Blackbeard along with eight of his men. They took the other nine back to Virginia for trial where they were convicted of piracy.

Following this conviction, the governor proceeded to send a member of the British Navy to the Pamlico area to recover the stolen goods, some of which were still in Tobias Knight's barn. Governor Eden and Colonel Thomas Pollock stood by Knight and remonstrated the governor of Virginia for invading North Carolina, even if it was to capture pirates.

At this time, although the records were public and were to be available for scrutiny, they were kept in private homes due to lack of public buildings. Thus when Maurice Moore and Edward Moseley desired to conduct a search of the records to determine exactly who was involved with Blackbeard, they had to break into a home. The governor was furious and issued a warrant for their arrest for breaking and entering and trespass. This led Moseley to make the statement that "the governor could find men enough to arrest peaceable citizens but none to arrest thieves and robbers," intimating that the governor was shielding the pirates.

At the Virginia trial, evidence was presented showing Knight to be associated with Teach. Knight, however, issued an explanation. He said that he had not concealed the fact that the sugar was stored in his barn, but that he had allowed Teach to store it there until the governor could find a more convenient place where the entire cargo could be stored. This implicated the governor.

The council declared Knight not guilty, but the circumstances surrounding his association with Teach were inconsistent with that innocence. At first Knight denied he had hidden any of the goods for Teach in his barn, but when told of a memo found on one of the dead pirates, he admitted the concealment. Not only was he accused of being a close associate of Blackbeard, his own correspondence with Teach, which began "my friend," and proceeded to give him advice, proved they were more than acquaintances. Thus nothing the governor or council could say helped Knight and he resigned his chief justice position and died before summer's end.

Recently, almost 300 hundred years after the incident, the wreckage of what is believed to be Blackbeard's ship the *Queen Anne's Revenge* was discovered by divers in the present Beaufort inlet between Shackelford Banks and Bogue Banks. Artifacts are being brought to the surface, cleaned, preserved, and displayed at the North Carolina Maritime Museum in Beaufort.

THE SPANISH INVASION

In the 1740s, Spanish privateers began roaming the coastal waters of North Carolina. At one point in 1741 they took possession of Ocracoke Inlet, seized ships coming into port, and were even so bold as to go ashore and take cattle from the inhabitants. They were eventually driven away, but the alarm was out to the government: The coastal towns were not set up to defend themselves. Yet nothing was done to fortify the various entrances to the state until later, after more incidents.

In 1747, the Spanish entered Beaufort harbor but were met by a small contingent of militia led by Major Enoch Ward who held them off until August 26. The Spanish possession of Beaufort was over by early September when Colonel Thomas Lovick and Captain Charles Cogdell gathered a greater number of militiamen and rid the town of the invaders.

The assembly passed a bill and money was raised to build two large forts at Cape Fear near Wilmington and at Ocracoke, the primary entrance to Pamlico Sound and the inland rivers to the towns.

Two smaller forts were to be built at Core Sound near Beaufort and Bear Inlet, between Beaufort and Wilmington, but the only one completed was at Cape Fear.

Blackbeard: The Capture of the Concorde *by Ann H. Hauman.*

The next summer, however, the Spanish were at it again, attacking the southern coast near Wilmington and Brunswick. Finally the Spanish were defeated, captured, or dead, the harassment of the coast of North Carolina was over.

Two years after the Spanish privateers were defeated in Brunswick, five Spanish vessels were lost in a great storm. One was beached near Topsail Inlet, the entrance to Beaufort; another near Drum Inlet on the Core Banks; and a third at Ocracoke. The other two sank off Currituck Inlet and Cape Hatteras.

In 1755, Governor Dobbs made a trip along the banks from Ocracoke Island down the Core Banks to Cape Lookout and Topsail Inlet. The harbor was used in the past by pirates, as well as by French and Spanish privateers for anchorage to gather wood and water and provide themselves with fresh meat and fish. It was a safe haven in strong ocean storms as well.

After touring the harbor at the cape the governor determined that it was a proper place to build a fort and a station for guardships and cruisers to do as the privateers had done: rest, repair, refresh, restock, and yet be able to be on the ocean quickly when necessary. The first fort built on the banks near Cape Lookout was called Fort Hancock.

THE REVOLUTION AND STATEHOOD

At the Provincial Council in 1775, Carteret County was represented by five men out of 184 who met in Hillsborough. By 1776, Cape Fear and the Chesapeake Bay were closed to shipping and Beaufort was frequently visited by British cruisers. Ocracoke, as it had been in the past, was the primary access to the Pamlico and Albemarle Sounds, as well as the rivers leading to the towns of Edenton, Washington, and New Bern. Merchants from these towns sent ships for cargoes of salt, powder, cannon, and munitions, as well as necessities for the public.

Privateers were going forth as well to intercept and plunder British vessels, and the state built armed cruisers for public service. For protection of the coast from Currituck to Cape Fear, five companies of troops were formed and stationed. There was a new system of militia with companies to be not less than 50 men, each to be divided into five divisions, one of which was the aged and infirm. Each county had field officers and the militia served only under the continental officers when ordered to. Districts included New Bern, with William Bryan as the general in charge, elected by congress.

A drawing of Hammock House, built c. 1709, by the author.

With regard to civilian lives, congress resolved that all vestries should proceed to parochial business and the care of the citizens of their parishes, especially the poor. They were also to conduct the business of the community. In Beaufort, Robert Williams set up a salt works on Gallants Point where pans from Philadelphia used to collect salt from seawater were erected. A conference with Benjamin Franklin of Pennsylvania provided Beaufort with the best way to process the salt. Others along the coastal areas began following the lead of Williams, as salt was a commodity necessary to the life of people in the colonies.

Congressmen from Carteret County declaring independence on April 12, 1776 were William Thomson, Solomon Shepard, and John Backhouse. On August 1 at Halifax the declaration of independence was read and proclaimed in every town and county. On August 9, the council prepared an address to the people recommending each county choose five delegates to represent them in writing the constitution for North Carolina.

James Davis of New Bern, a printer who had begun a newspaper in New Bern in 1755, printed copies to be sent to each county. Elections were held in October and congress met in November at Halifax with Richard Caswell as president. It was determined that a majority of the members were to govern rather than as before within counties. A committee was chosen to frame the constitution, with eastern members predominating until others arrived.

Temporary courts of Oyer and Terminer were established in several districts of the state. These courts were established to hear (oyer) and determine (terminer) cases that called for swift justice, such as horse thievery and counterfeiting. Two men learned in the law were appointed by the governor in each district. All statutes were consistent with freedom and independence and remained so until the next assembly. Regarding religious organizations, all property was to remain with the owners of the church, and ministers could celebrate marriages in their own church observing rules and regulations of the law. Courts of admiralty were also established and collectors of the customs appointed.

The governor was directed by the congress to offer free pardon and protection to anyone taking the oath of allegiance to the state within ten days. Those who did not were not allowed to bring suit, or purchase or transfer property. The first draft of the North Carolina constitution was given December 6. Following some discussion and a few changes, the constitution was adopted on December 18 and ordered printed and distributed.

Under the new constitution every county was entitled to one senator and two representatives. The legislature was divided into two houses, with a small number of members in each. During these times, things changed from the old ways to the new. Those who had previously had much power and influence in the government were no longer there. Each county now had equal representation.

By July 1777, many loyalists and their families had left North Carolina. British cruisers were attempting to close Ocracoke Inlet due to the importation of salt, ammunition, and other supplies, and privateers were still preying on the British ships. In November, the assembly met and established superior courts and courts

Collet's 1770 map of North Carolina. (Courtesy NC Department of Cultural Resources, Division of Archives and History.)

for trials of civil cases. New counties were named, a fort was built at Ocracoke, and commissioners were appointed to build a fort commanding the bay at Point Lookout. Academies were established and vestries were changed to overseers of the poor and to county wardens, a final separation of church and state.

In the 1780s, the assembly continued to meet annually, sometimes in Hillsborough, sometimes in New Bern, once in Smithfield because of the smallpox in New Bern, occasionally in Halifax, Wake County, Salem, and so forth. By 1783, naval stores such as tar, pitch, and turpentine were making a profit from export along with lumber and rice. Looms were busy, skins were tanned, otters and beaver provided fur, and shoemakers and hatters enjoyed trading. Nails were being made by hand, spinning jennies and hand weaving were in use, and cotton, linen, and woolen cloth was for sale. Corn and grain were in surplus, hogs and cattle were being raised, grain was converted to whiskey, and brandy was made from fruits in the orchards.

Justices continued to meet quarterly at the courthouses. Other gatherings at the courthouse, which was usually in the center of the community, were primarily to exchange news and views on a variety of issues, both family oriented, political, social, local, and far reaching.

But the century ended on a tragic note when disaster struck in 1798 in the form of yellow fever. It was rampant in Philadelphia and New York, and struck every seaport along the coast, including those of North Carolina.

6. Early Owners and Developers

The land that became Beaufort had many owners before it became a town. Each has a story to tell about Beaufort's way of life, the others who lived in the community, how the community was organized and run, and their own involvement in the growth of the new port. These families saw Beaufort through some rough times of little expansion, invasion by pirates and Spanish privateers, and even our own Revolution. But they survived, and partly because of their tenacity Beaufort has become what it is today. Some of their stories are told in the following pages.

Green

Farnival Green was one of the first to receive a grant from the lords proprietors. On December 20, 1707, he purchased 780 acres "beginning at the mouth of the Core River, running up the river and creek 245 poles to a pine, then east 345 poles to a gum, then north 80° east 45 poles to a pine at North River, then down the river to the mouth 420 poles, then along the sound to the first station." A pole is equal to 16.5 feet or 5.5 yards.

Evidently at about the same time, Peter Worden of the Pamlico River area was granted 640 acres on the west side of the North River, which overlapped Green's patent. In an agreement between them, a reference is made to "a point of land called Newport Town," which was apparently the site of the future Beaufort. It is possible there was already some settlement at this location, as in 1712 the Core River was renamed the Newport River.

Looking at early maps of the coastal area, it is difficult to tell exactly in today's measurements what Green's acreage encompassed. It is clear though that it was between the Core, or Newport, River and the North River and that it was on the Core Sound, which today is the present location of Beaufort Town.

Green, who lived on a plantation on the north side of the Neuse River, also received a grant for Craney Island, which was changed to Harkers Island later in the 1700s. Green served on the provincial assembly in 1709 and in 1711 requested assistance in defending the colonists from the hostile Native Americans. In addition, Green, with several others who are noted as developers of the Core

Sound community, petitioned to have a court in the Neuse River area so they would not have to travel such long and arduous journeys to Bath.

In a Native American attack on his plantation in 1714, Green was killed along with one of his sons, a white servant, and two African Americans. His widow later married Richard Graves, deputy surveyor, who prepared the first plan of the Town of Beaufort in 1713.

TURNER

Robert Turner lived and worked as a merchant in Bath. After purchasing the Core Sound property from Farnival Green in 1713, Turner set aside 100 of the 780 acres for the Town of Beaufort. The plat that was made then by Richard Graves is still in use today. In October Turner began selling lots in the town, although many of the titles lapsed for non-payment. Christopher Gale and Maurice Moore kept their lots, Gale owning half a block on the east side at the corner of Ann and Turner down to the water. Moore's lots were located between Ann and the water on the west side of Orange Street. Turner also sold part of his patent on North River to John Shackelford for "three gentle good cows and calves."

On October 19, 1720, Robert Turner sold the remainder of his 780 acres, including the Town of Beaufort, to Richard Rustull of Carteret Precinct for £150. He returned to the Pamlico area and later represented Beaufort County in the colonial assembly and represented Bath Town in 1738–1739 and 1742–1744.

RUSTULL, OR RUSSELL

Richard Rustull Sr. was born in 1669 to William and Ann Austin Rustull, who had settled in Bath County early in the 1700s. He married Margaret Bell, the daughter of John and Margaret Blish Bell.

On October 19, 1720, Rustull purchased 780 acres on Core Sound, except for the lots previously granted, from Robert Turner for £150. He was one of the first justices of the peace, a vestryman, the tax collector, a town commissioner, and the treasurer. It was during his ownership that the town was named a port in 1722 and the seat of government for Carteret Precinct in 1723. When the town was incorporated in 1723, Rustull increased its size to 200 acres.

In 1724, Rustull sold an unidentified lot to St. John's Parish with a building that was to be used as the courthouse and the church. According to legend, the building burned in 1725 and was totally blown down by a hurricane the next year. With the loss of a meeting place, the justices and commissioners used the Hammock House, which was then owned by Rustull.

A year later Rustull sold the township for £500 to Nathaniel Taylor. A deed described the township as extending "100 yards eastward of ye hammock that Thomas Austin formerly lived on," which according to the Moseley map of 1733 shows the "I. Taylor" house. This was possibly the earliest house built in the area and was used as a guide to seamen entering the channel at the west end of Cart

Many of Beaufort's early developers are buried in the old burying ground. (Photo by Diane Hardy.)

Island to Old Topsail Inlet and into the harbor. The deed also identifies the house as being on a "rich hummock" with land to the northeast belonging to R. Rustull.

In 1736, Richard Rustull Jr. married Mary Stanton, the daughter of Henry Stanton Sr., a Quaker living in the Core Creek area. A year later, Stanton gave to "his loving son, planter" 100 acres adjoining his plantation, where they lived.

DENNIS

William Dennis was an inn keeper from England, as well as an associate of Richard Rustull Jr. in ocean shipping. When Dennis married Richard Jr.'s widow, she had inherited a small house with outbuildings located on lot 13 in Old Town, at the corner of Craven Street and the waterfront. The house, originally a story and a jump, was designed and built by shipwrights using the available space most effectively and making it capable of withstanding storms. It was enlarged over time and eventually became the townhouse of the Dennis family. It was also used as an ordinary.

69

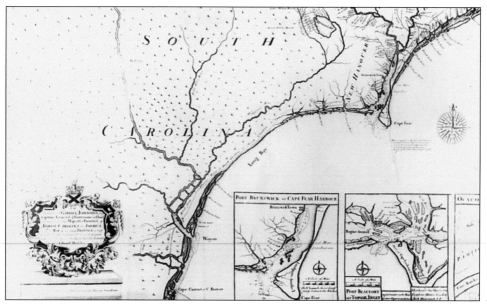

A map of Clarendon County, South Carolina, with inset showing the port of Beaufort. (Courtesy NC Department of Cultural Resources, Division of Archives and History.)

In the twentieth century the house was moved twice. First around the corner on Craven Street to make room for modern commercial buildings, and finally to the grounds of the Beaufort Historical Association, where it resides today as the Mattie King Davis Art Gallery.

Dennis built a gambrel-roof house on Bogue Sound west of Broad Creek in 1760. He was part of the militia, serving during the Spanish invasion. During the Revolution he served as a major and was the sheriff between 1784 and 1791. His son William Jr. was in the Continental Line in 1776–1778, retiring as a captain. William Jr. never married, living with his father until 1790, when they quarreled and the son moved out. William Dennis died in 1802.

TAYLOR

Nathaniel Taylor purchased the 200 acres of Beaufort Township on December 15, 1725 from Richard Rustull Sr. He paid £500 and extended the township 100 yards east of the hammock on which Thomas Austin had lived and which included the Hammock House. The channel ran from this point by the west end of Cart Island to Old Topsail Inlet.

In 1731, Taylor donated a lot in the center of town to be used as a burial ground. This is part of the Old Burying Ground today. He also bought 200 acres on the east side of the White Oak River. In 1733, he was a justice of the peace and court again met at his house, although a new courthouse was built in 1728. On October 2, 1733, he sold his interest in the town of Beaufort to Thomas Martin of South

River, in Craven County. Taylor's Creek, flowing along Front Street of Beaufort, was named for Nathaniel Taylor.

A year later Taylor made his will, which was witnessed by Francis Davis, and he died shortly thereafter, with his wife, Jane, following in days. Davis had also written her will, which left the estate to Nathaniel's "faithful servant" Ismael Taylor, thus the I. Taylor on Moseley's map.

MARTIN

Thomas Martin purchased the 200 acres of Beaufort Township on October 2, 1733 for £500. Witnesses of the sale were Thomas Lovick, James Winwright (the clerk of court), and Samuel Turner. In 1739, he sold the property to John Pinder, but retained 2 acres east of Stansbury Gut on Taylor's Creek where he had a wharf. He deeded half-acre lots in 1743 to Sarah and Ann Bonner, who were spinsters. Apparently they did not claim the lots, as they reverted back to Pinder, who sold them to Robert Williams in 1757.

Martin died in 1758 leaving his wife with his property, which included 2,000 acres at South River and 1,400 acres at Lukens.

PINDER

John Pinder was a mariner from Philadelphia. On May 25, 1739, he purchased Beaufort Town from Thomas Martin for the phenomenally low price of £60. Pinder attempted to have the name of the creek in front of his property changed from Taylor's to Pinder's Creek, but he was unsuccessful.

Evidently he was not doing any better with the town than the earlier purchasers, for in three years he sold the property to James Winwright for £500 and moved to New Bern where he became a merchant.

WINWRIGHT

James Winwright, the next owner of the town of Beaufort, came to Albemarle County from New England before 1722. He was a member of the assembly from Pasquotank, a juror, provost marshall under Governor Burrington, and a man of means.

In 1725, he and his wife, Ann, settled on a plantation he called Newfoundland on the north side of the Newport River at Deep Run. He became a justice of the peace, surveyor, county treasurer, clerk of court, vestryman, and town commissioner. He also began acquiring property within Beaufort. On June 1, 1731, he purchased lot 10 from the town fathers, and in 1742, he purchased the 200 acres comprising the town, except for those lots that had sold previously.

There is a wonderful story tied to lot 10 that was written by Jean B. Kell, a local historian, called "Love, Goodwill and Affection." The story was turned into a musical and performed in Beaufort several years ago.

Winwright died in 1744, leaving his property to his wife. His personal items and books were left with George Read, another clerk of court and the vestry. Thomas Lovick and George Read were executors to his will.

Winwright directed in his will that with the rents and profits of his land and houses in Beaufort, the chairman of the Carteret County Court along with a church warden of St. John's Parish, should find a "sober discreet qualified man to teach a school, at least Reading Writing Vulgar and Decimal Arithmetick," in the town of Beaufort. They were also ordered to build a schoolhouse and provide land as the Church of England did for its ministers.

Although there is no information about the construction of this first public school in North Carolina, there is evidence that it was built and used. As early as 1745 there was a school in Straits, a community about 7 miles "downeast" of Beaufort on the mainland. A young school teacher from New England named Rachel Young arrived there and lived in the home of Samuel Chadwick. She later married Samuel's son Thomas Chadwick.

It was at the school in Beaufort township in 1782 that the leaders of the local militia met to negotiate with the British when they invaded the town. This building was burned down at their departure. It is possible that the schoolhouse shows on the 1770 Sauthier map to the east of the main part of Beaufort.

LOVICK

The Lovicks were indeed good friends of the Winwrights, who apparently had no children. John and Thomas Lovick were sons of Sir Edward Lovick of London. In 1710, they joined some Welsh Quakers who attempted a settlement on Clubfoot and Hancock Creeks near the Neuse River. John was apparently an attorney and assumed an important role in the colonial government in Edenton. When Tobias Knight was forced to leave the position of secretary, John took his place.

John was married first to the daughter of John and Elizabeth Davis Blount. His second wife was a widow and the daughter of Governor Eden. When the governor died in 1721, John was his heir and executor. It was during Eden's term that John acquired Ocracoke Island. He served on the commission to lay out the boundary between Virginia and North Carolina and died in 1733 leaving no children. Part of his estate went to his brother Thomas and his nephew John, Thomas's son.

In 1722, Thomas served as secretary of the receiver general and, in 1732, was appointed collector of customs at the Port of Beaufort. He also purchased 720 acres along the Newport River as well as lots 16, 17, 18, 52, and 62 in the Old Town. These lots comprise the half-block on the east side of Turner Street, between Anne Street and the waterfront.

In 1734, Thomas represented Carteret County in the colonial assembly with James Winwright, and in 1736, he was the head of the county court of common pleas and quarter sessions. From 1735 to 1746, he was a representative of Carteret County in the colonial assembly with Arthur Mabson, and in 1746 William Borden was to be his associate in the assembly but he refused to take the oath, and it was Joseph Bell who went with Thomas instead. In 1742, Thomas was a vestryman of St. John's Parish, and he served as a colonel in the local militia during the invasion of the Spanish pirates in 1747.

Thomas died in 1761, but as a member of the provincial assembly he was instrumental in securing authorization to fortify the coastal towns. At his death, Sarah made a prenuptial agreement with William Heritage of Craven County. She died prior to 1769, and William's legatee was Anna, the wife of George Phenney Lovick. In 1765, George Phenney disposed of the property he had inherited from his father, selling all the Beaufort lots to Joseph Bell Jr., a tailor.

AUSTIN

Thomas Austin Sr. was a vestryman of St. John's Parish as well as justice of the peace and juryman. He had a close relationship with the Rustull family. One of his wives, Lydia, was the widow of William Rustull, the brother of Richard Sr.

In 1724, Thomas bought 26 acres called "ye Indian Towne" on the west side of the Newport River from Charles Cogdell. Thomas was a cooper, and was active in county affairs. His son Thomas Jr., a collector at the Port of Beaufort, married Rebecca Physioc in 1725, the oldest daughter of John Physioc.

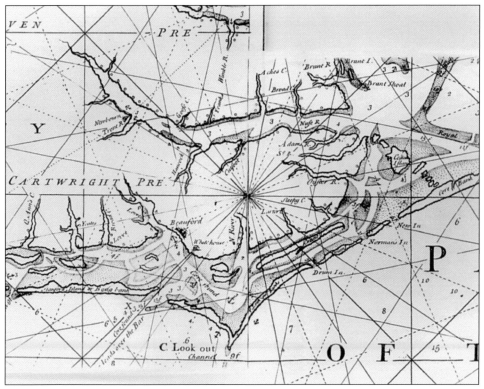

Wimble's 1738 map of "Cartwright Pre." showing "Beauford" and the "white house."

By 1745, Thomas Sr. was living on a plantation on the south side of the Newport River. In 1747, he was a member of the local militia under Major Enoch Ward and Captain Charles Cogdell during the Spanish invasion. In 1751, he purchased land on the White Oak River and apparently lived there. He was named a lay reader on Pettiford's Creek and Bogue Sound in 1761 and moved to Craven County in 1768. He died in 1778, leaving his property to his wife, Mary.

BELL

Much of the Bell family's history has already been assembled elsewhere. Originally from Nansemond County in Virginia, John Bell and his wife, Mary, lived in Pasquotank County where John was a vestryman at St. Peter's Parish. On his death, John Bell left all his land at Alligator River to his son James. His land on the north side of the Pasquotank River he left to his sons John, William Ross, George, and Nathaniel.

James Bell may have remained in Pasquotank where he married Mary Billet, daughter of John and Alice Billet. They had a son Newell Bell, and moved to Carteret County. Throughout their lives James and Newell were active in the court, serving as jurymen at various times and as road overseers.

A drawing of the Josiah Bell house, built c. 1825, by the author.

John Bell married Margaret Blish in the Currituck area. They had a daughter Margaret who married Richard Rustull Sr., the son of William and Ann Austin Rustull. Both Rustull Sr. and Austin Sr. were vestrymen of St. John's Parish and justices in the court of Carteret Precinct.

In 1756, John Bell was authorized by the vestry of St. John's Parish to employ a schoolmaster to keep school two years, including the schools at Shepard's Neck and Straits. Shepard's Neck is an area of Morehead City where Bogue Sound and the Newport River meet. The school year was three months. In 1765, the vestry was seeking to employ three school teachers.

George Bell signed a petition in 1712 to hold court in New Bern since Bath was so far away and there was no room for the people from New Bern to stay when court was in session. In 1712–1713, the Court of Craven bound Charles and George Cogdaile (Cogdell) to George Bell to be taught to read and write. If this George was the son of John and Mary Bell, and the brother of James, John, William Ross, Nathaniel, Henry, Joseph, Benjamin, and Mary, he may never have lived in Carteret.

The George Bell who lived in Carteret was the son of William Ross and Martha Bell and a brother of Ross, Joseph, and Mary Bell. In 1752, he was granted administration of his mother, Martha Bell Howland's estate.

William Ross Bell, known as Ross, acquired land on the White Oak River in 1714. In 1723, he was the plaintiff in a suit in the court. In 1724, he was accused of bodily harm by Robert Atkins and in turn sued Atkins. In the 1725 court he was shown as a jurist. He also recorded a deed of 689 acres in 1725. He served as jury foreman and was the plaintiff in another suit. In September 1726, his last will and testament was presented at court with his brother Joseph Bell shown as executor.

As with the George Bells, there were also many juniors and seniors among the Joseph Bells. Joseph Sr. was the brother of James, John, William Ross, etc. and the son of John and Mary. He was married to Margaret Bell and their children were Elizabeth, Thomas, and Prudence Bell Stephens.

Joseph Sr. was granted part of the same land in Currituck that his brother Andrew had acquired on July 27, 1708. On September 7, 1725, he was granted guardianship of two of Andrew's sons, George, age 16, and Josiah, age 14, after they petitioned the court to be indentured to him. Joseph Sr. lived in Carteret, was an attorney, an early court justice, and signed an act of assembly in 1723 to settle titles and bounds of lands. On February 22, 1713, he acquired 370 acres on the White Oak River adjoining the lands of his brother Ross Bell.

Joseph Jr. was the other son of Andrew Bell, Joseph Sr.'s brother. He was born in 1695 and was the most prominent member of the Bell family, but he was called Junior until his uncle's death in 1745, when he became both Joseph Sr. and colonel. Although he owned land in Carteret, he lived in Norfolk County, Virginia. He moved to Carteret in 1736 and purchased land on the Newport Sound from Christopher Dudley. In 1739, he sold part of his Virginia property, and the rest he devised to his son Andrew in his will of 1775. In turn, Andrew passed this property on to his son Lovett in his 1790 will.

As an aside, Joseph Bell Jr. was married to Mary Corbett and they had five sons: Church, who was married to Sarah Shepard, daughter of David Shepard, and died in 1775; Andrew, who married Elizabeth Lovett, daughter of John Lovett, and moved to New Bern in 1787; Caleb, who married Susannah Coale, daughter of Captain William Coale; Joseph, who was married first to Hannah Lovett, daughter of John Lovett, and then to Jane Davis; and Malachi, who also married twice, first to Elizabeth Coale, daughter of William Coale, and second to Sarah, daughter of Joseph Fulford and widow of George Robertson.

In 1741, Joseph became a justice in Carteret County and held the position for 36 years, with occasional breaks to hold other offices. From 1748 to 1760 and again in 1764 and 1765 he was a member of the North Carolina legislature representing Carteret County. Joseph served in 1746 with Thomas Lovick in the colonial assembly until 1761 when Lovick died. On December 4, 1749, Joseph purchased a 640-acre tract on the north side of the Newport River, joining the westernmost side of Deep Creek, across the creek, and another 560 acres on the north side of the Newport River at the mouth of Black Creek. This was from the estate of James Winwright through Thomas Lovick and George Read, executors.

In 1752, Joseph became a vestryman of St. John's Parish in Carteret County. He also served as a lieutenant colonel and later colonel of the Carteret County militia. On January 10, 1755, he purchased from James Smith of Craven County 240 acres on the north side of the Newport River beginning at Shepards. In 1767, he sold 120 acres of this property to John Simmons.

On May 20, 1755, Joseph gave to the church wardens of St. John's Parish 30 square yards of land "near the road leading to White Oak River, and to the westward of Major David Shepard's plantation where he now lives . . . to take in and encompass a new chapel which is now abuilding." This chapel, known as Bell's Chapel, became a Methodist church after the Revolution. Grave stones from the Bell family still rest in the yard where the chapel stood.

In 1757, Joseph Bell became a commissioner for the town of Portsmouth, and in 1766, he received a license to keep an ordinary in Beaufort. In Joseph Bell's will his children were all given land and slaves, as well as household property. To his grandson David Bell, son of Church Bell, he gave his house and lot 19, plus the south half of lot 53 with the house on it built for the registrar's office.

Lot 19 stands on the west side of Turner Street running 330 feet north from the edge of Taylor's Creek. The house that has been known for more than 30 years as "the red house" is more properly known as the Joseph Bell house. Legend has it that this was Joseph Bell's town house, where he would come when serving in the court, and for town meetings and church services. It belongs to the historic association and is currently undergoing an enormous restoration project. Lot 53 is just north of lot 19, and today is nothing but a parking lot. There is no sign of any small building or house that might have been the registrar's office.

It is interesting to note, however, that in the 1770s Claude Joseph Sauthier, a surveyor and mapmaker, mapped the town of Beaufort from the water, and this block between Taylor's Creek, Orange Street, Anne Street, and Turner Street appeared to be the center of town. The map shows several buildings clustered in the center of the area that eventually formed the block and one of them was most likely the registrar's office.

The Bells were notable throughout the entire eighteenth century and into the 1800s. Brothers, children, grandchildren, and great grandchildren all continued using the same family names such as Joseph, George, and Malachi, while at the same time adding other names from the Fishers, Coales, Lovetts, and others with whom they married.

BORDEN

The Borden family is interesting as well, in that—as the story goes—they were the progenitors of the Borden Milk Company. William F. Borden, son of John and Mary Earle Borden, was born August 15, 1689 in Portsmouth, Rhode Island. On July 7, 1715, he married Alice Hull of Jamestown, Rhode Island, and in 1732, the family sailed to North Carolina and settled on the north side of the Newport River.

The Bordens, with the Stantons, established a settlement in what is known today as the Mill Creek area and began building ships for the people up north.

A drawing of the Joseph Bell house, built c. 1767, by the author.

Large numbers of workers came from Rhode Island to work on the ships and do the logging. Not only did William Borden build ships, he was also well known for the manufacture of duck material from flax that was used in making sails.

In 1746, William was elected a member of the North Carolina general assembly but declined to be sworn in as he was a Quaker. He and his wife, Alice Hull Borden, a sister of Mary Hull Stanton, had four daughters, Alice, Katherine, Hope, and Hannah, and one son, William Jr.

Hannah married John Mace in 1756. In 1774, he purchased a plantation at Core Creek, near the Core Sound Meeting House. Their daughter Sarah married Jonas Small and had nine children.

William Jr. married Comfort Lovett. He became a successful planter and was a delegate to the first provincial congress at Halifax, North Carolina in 1775, to resolve independence from England. In 1788, he was elected to the general assembly in Hillsborough, North Carolina, when the constitution of the state was written and adopted, and where North Carolina, after insisting on the Bill of Rights, joined the new American nation. By 1790, William Jr. was the largest slave owner in Carteret County.

The type of house built by the Stanton and Borden families when they arrived in Carteret County in the 1730s.

On William Borden Sr.'s death in 1748, William Jr. inherited the "dwelling house and manor plantation" with all the old patent land, and 800 acres to be laid out by his executors as Harlowe Creek. He left many acres of land on Bogue Banks to be divided among his children and grandchildren. The one exception to his generosity was his daughter Sarah, to whom he left one shilling as she had been "undutiful and married William Pratt against [Borden's] own and all her friends consent."

In 1782, the British had entered Beaufort, come ashore, and destroyed the schoolhouse. Before their departure from the area had sailed up the Newport River to Borden's shipyard, where they burned everything and took away some of the slaves.

COGDELL, OR COGDAILE

Charles Cogdell and his brother George came to Carteret County and Beaufort prior to 1713 and were indentured to George Bell, who had requested of Governor Eden that he keep them so they could learn "ye building of vessels" and to read and write.

In 1713, George Cogdell patented land on Shepard's Point that was transferred from Sarah Porter. By 1722, Charles and George began acquiring land in Carteret County. Charles became a member of the first vestry of St. John's Parish and was appointed a commissioner of peace in 1727. Both Charles and George served as justices of the peace.

In 1723, Charles was named by the court to oversee laying out a bridle path from his plantation to the White Oak River. In 1724, he sold 26 acres known as "Ye Indian Towne" on the west side of the Newport River to Thomas Austin Sr. Charles also represented Carteret County in the provincial assembly of 1733 and, in 1747, was a captain in the local militia during the Spanish invasion. His brother George served as well, and his son Richard was an ensign.

Charles's son Richard was born in Beaufort in 1724. He was a deputy sheriff before 1748, and then moved to Johnston County where he established a mercantile business. In 1756, he went to New Bern where he continued his business and also ran an ordinary. He served as a justice, sheriff, and member of the assembly.

In 1766, Richard Cogdell represented Carteret County in the assembly, where he introduced and obtained approval to build a canal connecting Clubfoot and Harlowe's Creek. It would be more than 40 years before this came to be.

By 1771, he was a lieutenant colonel in the militia and participated in the Battle of Alamance against the Regulators, members of several bands organized in North Carolina to resist official extortion. As a close friend of Governor Tryon he became a strong advocate of independence and represented Craven County in the first three provincial congresses in New Bern and Halifax.

He was the judge of admiralty court in Beaufort in 1775–1776, and in 1778–1779 represented New Bern in the state house of commons.

DAVIS

The name Davis is well known in Beaufort and Carteret County. William Davis, born in 1692, was the son of James Davis and Elizabeth White. Their ancestry goes back at least to 1607 when William's great-great grandfather sailed from Wales and landed in Jamestown. It is unclear whether he remained or returned to Wales.

According to family history, William himself came to this country in 1700 from Wales and, in 1715, arrived in Carteret County. In 1728, he was asked by the commissioners to build a new courthouse/church on the same site as the original that had burned and then been totally destroyed in a hurricane.

Another source, however, claims he came to this area in 1736, having been a carpenter in Perquimans. It was there he knew Joseph Wicker, having served with him as local official for the Albemarle region. He sold his lands there and secured a patent for land in Carteret.

Davis married Mary Wicker, the daughter of Joseph and Ruth Wicker. Mary had been given an island in Core Sound by her father who had been clerk of court in 1725 and 1726 and a member of the legislature in 1733. The name of Davis Island, the site of the Davis family home, continues today.

William was a very devoted member of the Church of England and served as a lay reader, and also as chief justice for the county. His home on Davis Island was surrounded by live oaks and cedars and contained rich soil. Jarrett's Bay to the west supplied the family with oysters while Davis Shore to the east was the farm. To the south were ducks and geese and all sorts of fish. His farm area was used for services, and as one story has it, his friends and neighbors would row over from Smyrna and Straits, be met by his family, and join together in listening to the sermons under the shade of the old oaks. They would then all gather around the table filled with food and drink.

William died in 1756, leaving his wife, Mary, one daughter, and eight sons, with sons Nathan and Joseph as executors of his will. The other children were Wicker, Caleb, William, Solomon White, Isaac, Benjamin, and Abigail. These sons were all on the vestry of St. John's Parish during their lives.

Nathan Davis was a member of the county court from 1756 to 1760 and was reappointed in 1760 by the governor, but declined to serve. He owned large amounts of property including Jarrett's Bay, which he gave to his son Isaiah, who passed it along to his sons Anthony and Samuel. Anthony Davis, born in 1779, gave a half-acre of land to the people of Core Sound, North River, and Straits for a church in 1829.

It is believed that Wicker and Isaac left the county after the Revolutionary War, taking their families to some distant land unknown to the family historians. Solomon White died in 1794 leaving his widow, Jean, six sons, and five daughters.

Benjamin Davis, the youngest son of William and Mary, married Sabra Williston and had 11 children. Benjamin fought in the Revolutionary War, left the Church

A drawing of the third courthouse, built in 1796, by the author. William Davis built the second courthouse in 1728.

of England, and became a Baptist. He died in 1814, leaving four sons and seven daughters. His son Whittington was a member of the house of commons in 1816 and a state senator from 1821 to 1816. Another son Thomas Clifford was born in 1775 and married Mary David Foote in 1803, the daughter of Lieutenant David Foote and Hepsabeth Bell Foote.

FISHER

The Fisher family of Carteret County and Beaufort began in 1741 with the birth of William Fisher. In 1768, he married Charity Pacquinet of Beaufort. They had six children, the most prominent of whom was William Jr., who married Catherine Fuller, daughter of Mary Pacquinet and Nathan Fuller. William Jr. and Catherine had three children, two of whom only lived about a month.

When Sarah Fisher married John Jones, her father gave her 70 acres on Shepard's Point. Following Jones's death and her marriage to Bridges Arendell, she and Bridges built their home on this land in 1834. The property today is part of Morehead City, and Fisher Street and Arendell Street are named for these two families.

Christopher Gale, the first chief justice of Carolina.

William Fisher had purchased a great amount of acreage, which was distributed to his children and grandchildren. He bequeathed to his wife, Charity, the plantation where they lived, the dwelling house, outhouses, tools, household goods and furniture, animals, and slaves, plus the grist mill and house on a half-acre lot in Beaufort he had purchased from John Rumley.

FULFORD

The Fulford family originally came from London to Barbados in 1635. Joseph Fulford Sr., born in 1690, came to America from Barbados and in 1708 was granted 520 acres on the Pamlico River. He patented land at Straits in 1714 and in 1719 was granted 130 acres on Core Sound at the west side of Nelson's Creek. He also had other grants and purchases. In 1723, he was serving on the vestry of St. John's Parish.

In 1740, Joseph Fulford Jr., born in 1725, was granted 350 acres by George II at the head of Fulford's Creek in Straits.

GALE

Christopher Gale is best known as the chief justice of the province. He was the son of Miles Gale, and his brother Edmund was one of the first to patent land in the Carteret County area.

In 1711, Christopher Gale was the receiver general of the province and was sent to Charleston to solicit aid. On the return voyage, bringing ammunition, he was captured and taken prisoner by the French and detained several months. On his eventual return he was appointed colonel of the militia for Bath County.

An act of the Carolina assembly in 1715 divided Pampticough Parish into Saint Thomas Parish, Hyde Parish, and Craven Parish. Gale was one of the original lot owners in Bath and he kept his permanent home at a plantation called "Kirby Grange."

Bath was the only town in the parish and was accessible by water, but had no church. Kirby Grange became a meeting place for worship until the St. Thomas church was built in 1734. Vestrymen were appointed in 1715, among them Charles Eden, governor from 1714 to 1722; Christopher Gale; and Tobias Knight, who also owned property in Carteret Precinct.

Gale was with John Lawson when the German Palatines came to this country. He became involved with de Graffenried and Lawson in the settling of New Bern and the Neuse River area. Luck was with him during the venture to Native American country when de Graffenried and Lawson were captured by the natives, and Lawson was killed. Christopher's wife had taken sick and he was unable to go with them.

On October 17, 1713, Christopher Gale purchased lots 16, 17, 18, 52, and 62 from Robert Turner. The property that Edmund Gale had patented is today known as Gale's Creek. In 1715, Edmund sold that patent to Christopher who later deeded it to his daughter Elizabeth Clayton.

In the summer of 1717, Christopher sailed to London, was reappointed by the lords proprietors as chief justice and returned to the Carolinas four years later when Governor Eden died.

In addition to resuming his official duties Gale took a seat on the council board as deputy to James Bertie, one of the lords proprietors. He became a most respected and influential member of the opposition to the new governor.

Gale became the first collector of customs at Port Beaufort in 1722–1723. He also served as a town commissioner and was one of the first wardens of the newly established St. John's Parish of the Church of England.

He returned to Bath and in 1724, he was collector of customs for Port Currituck in the northeastern part of the province. He continued as collector of customs and chief justice until 1731, when he moved to the Cape Fear area, having been at odds with several governors during that time.

Gale's will stated that he was "born at York in the Kingdom of Great Britain, but now Collector of his Majesty's Customs at the port of Roanoak."

LEFFERS

Samuel Leffers, born in 1736, was a late-comer to Beaufort and Carteret County. He arrived in 1764 from Hempstead, New York and in 1766 married Sarah Hampton, the daughter of Thomas Hampton, a local shoemaker. In 1775, he purchased lot 12 in New Town and built a small house. He also purchased lot 48 in Old Town, which became the home of his daughter Mary Ann and her husband, John Dill. In 1778, he sold lot 12 in New Town. In 1790, he signed a nine-year lease with William Borden covering 170 acres that Borden owned at Gallants Point and five years later he purchased the property on the hummock, including the house and windmill.

Leffers was a schoolmaster, planter, surveyor, town official, and merchant. One of his most prominent and valuable jobs was as clerk of court and clerk of the vestry for St. John's Parish. It is through his detailed note-taking and meticulous handwriting that we have access today to records of Beaufort's past.

Leffers and his wife had five children. After Sarah died in 1808, he sold the property in Beaufort and moved to Straits where he spent his last years living with his grandson Samuel. The grandfather was a prolific letter writer and produced many documents that are preserved to this day. One of Leffers's letters says that mail service between New Bern and Beaufort was only "fortnightly," or every two weeks, in 1802. In 1803, he wrote that a storm in late August sank or damaged boats in the harbor and destroyed houses and blew down chimneys.

In 1809, Leffers notes the death of his wife and the building of Fort Hampton. An 1812 letter tells of the alarm of war and the battalions of local militia posted in Beaufort and at Fort Hampton. By 1814, his grandson Samuel had volunteered for service at Fort Hampton because the regulars had been ordered to Canada. He also mentioned that there was finally inland water transportation between Beaufort Inlet and Virginia.

NELSON

The Nelson family has a wonderfully rich history that began when Captain John Nelson Jr. sailed into Bath County, North Carolina. He had 12 colonists on board his ship including his father, three sisters, and his wife, Ann A. Nelson. The lords proprietors had advertised in England with an offer of 50 acres to the provider of passage for each colonist brought to North Carolina.

In 1702, Captain Nelson filed an entry of land in Bath County, acquiring 600 acres in Hunting Quarters, known today as Sea Level. He was required to occupy and use the land or it would be forfeited.

He and his wife acquired large tracts of land on the north and south sides of the Neuse River where they had several orchards. Most of the time they stayed at the plantation, which was on the north side of the Neuse in Craven County, but they also had a smaller plantation on the south side near Garbacon Creek in Carteret Precinct.

Nelson played an important role in the early history of Carteret Precinct, having signed a petition in 1712 asking that the court be held in this area and serving as a member of the first vestry of St. John's Parish.

When Nelson's first wife Ann died, he married Mary Lewis and provided her with rights to one-half of the Hunting Quarters property for her lifetime. They had no children themselves, although she had three from a previous marriage. In 1746, Captain Nelson gave his son James all of the Hunting Quarters plantation, reserving the homeplace and one-half of the land for him and his wife during their lifetime.

Nelson's other son Thomas died before 1752, leaving a wife and two sons. Captain Nelson, in concern for his son's widow and his grandchildren, transferred 540 acres at Garbacon Creek to the grandsons, appointing their uncle as overseer. Instructions were also given that their mother was to receive one-third of the profit from the orchards and grounds for her lifetime.

In 1759, Thomas Nelson's son Thomas Jr. came of age and gave his little brother John Jr. 450 acres. Family history says John Jr. never married and died in his early 40s. Thomas Jr. built a good shipping business and had a prosperous plantation prior to his death in early 1800. It is also apparent that Thomas Jr. must have married and had a grandson named John Hancock Nelson, born in 1814.

©Maurice™ 1984   The Leffers House · 1778 · Restoration Grounds· Beaufort ·NC

A drawing of the Leffers house, built c. 1778, by the author.

After the death of his first wife, John Hancock Nelson married Mehitabel Mason of Adams Creek, who was born in 1831. They lived on the Garbacon Creek plantation, although John Hancock owned a house in New Bern. According to family records, the couple decided to move to Beaufort to provide better educational opportunities for their children. Although now labeled as the "Nelson House, c. 1790," it is said that the house at the corner of Moore and Front Streets was built by James Davis and purchased in 1875 by John Hancock Nelson for $2,000.

John Hancock Nelson died in 1876 and is buried in the Old Burying Ground in Beaufort. His widow Hettie inherited the Beaufort house and lived there until her death in 1917. Her daughter Laura married Thomas Duncan in 1881. That couple inherited the Nelson house and sold it to Joseph House in 1922. The house today is called the "House house."

READ AND RUSSELL, OR RUSTULL

Three generations of Reads were prominent in the courts and vestry, serving as clerks to both. George Read was clerk of court from June 1741 to March 1755 and was also clerk of the vestry of St. John's Parish from at least 1743 to 1754. When he died in September 1755, his son Robert followed him in the same positions but resigned as clerk of the vestry in 1790 due to consumption. Robert's son George was later chosen to be the clerk of the wardens of the poor, the former office of vestry.

Nancy Ann Read, daughter of Robert and his wife, Esther, married John Rustull and is buried with him in the Russell family cemetery near Core Creek. Rustull was a member of the assembly, legislator, justice of the peace, and Revolutionary War soldier. He was 64 when he died in 1802.

His son John Russell II was born in January 1769 and died in October 1860. John Russell III, his son, was born in May 1806, married Catherine Oglesby in 1832, and died in 1879. He was a licensed minister, justice of the peace, and the sheriff. Catherine was a schoolteacher. In 1832–1833, they built a church house and school building.

SHACKELFORD

Prior to 1712, John Shackelford was a signer of the petition to the government in Bath requesting that a court be held in the Neuse River area. He had come to Bath County with his brother Francis and, in 1708, patented a plantation on the west side of North River. From 1712 to 1733, John served in the local militia. He is listed as a vestryman in the vestry book of St. John's Parish from 1723 through 1733. In 1712, his garrison at the Shackelford Plantation was to be allowed "to plant corne on sd plantation, plant, tend and gather corne during time they keep a garrison there," according to the Carteret County Historical Society's *Heritage of Carteret County*. Troops stationed at the garrison were expected to take care of this.

The Nelson house, built c. 1790. (Courtesy Beaufort Historical Association.)

In 1713, Shackelford purchased part of Robert Turner's patent on North River above Turner's Creek, as well as 7,000 acres known as Sea Banks, a part of the outer banks in Carteret County. He was also appointed to see "every ship drawing 8-feet of water anchoring at the banks and Shackelford Banks to charge three shillings six pence per foot."

Enoch Ward came to Carteret about the same time, as he and Shackelford purchased the Banks together from John Porter. Their division gave Enoch the Core Banks section while John retained the western part, which is still known as Shackelford Banks.

Shackelford married Ann Levingston and they had at least eight children. In his 1734 will, he gave his daughters Mary, Elizabeth, and Ann each a gold ring. To his daughter Sarah he gave four cows and calves, and to his son Joseph he gave the liberty to build a house and shop on the island where he had been living. He also gave Joseph liberty to "whaile off ye banks," paying to his widow Ann the "rent of two barrells of oyle for his share of one half of one single boat and to have the liberty of no more boats or part of my boats."

To his grandsons, John and William Roberts, Shackelford gave cows and calves and his daughter Hannah was to receive a large cedar cubbard and round table as well as pewter plates, a feather bed blanket, and cotton sheets. Another son James and his heirs forever were to receive property on the banks east of Old Topsail Inlet called Shackelford Banks, plus Carrot Island. The remaining son

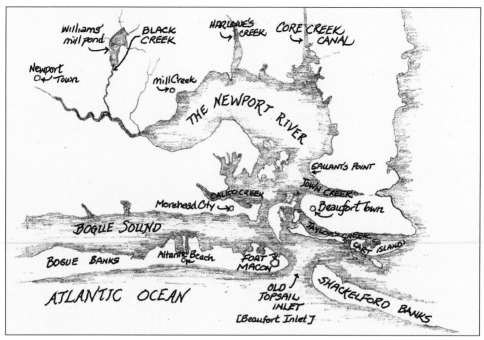

A map of the area settled in the early 1700s, by the author.

John Shackelford Jr., who served in 1747 with the local militia when the Spanish invaded Beaufort, was to have all the goods not given to the others after the death of his mother.

SHEPARD

The Shepard name is more closely associated with the area of Carteret County known today as Morehead City, but the family was also important in the history of Beaufort.

In 1723, David Shepard bought 170 acres from John Shackelford at the mouth of the Newport River bounded by Bogue Sound on the south and Calico Creek on the north. The son of Thomas Shepard, David came from Virginia, settled in Beaufort, married, and bought property along the Newport River in the Mill Creek area as well as in today's Newport town, which was known as Shepardsville during the Civil War. David was also a merchant, ship builder, and plantation owner.

In April 1752, the vestry minutes of St. John's Parish record the qualification of David Shepard Jr., who was chosen church warden. There is some confusion in the sequence of David Shepards, for in May 1754 the vestry minutes recorded an item to the effect that Major David Shepard rendered an account for his deceased son David Shepard, a former church warden. This tends to suggest that his father did not die in 1748 but in 1775 as other information states.

In his will of 1774, Shepard gave his sons Solomon and Elijah the point of land known first as Read's Neck, then as Shepard's Point, and today as Morehead City. William Shepard, a grandson of David, later came into possession of the Read's Neck property plus adjoining acreage, where he built his home plantation. In 1791, he sold the 600 acres from the mouth of the Newport River west to William Fisher.

THOMSON

William Thomson was a mariner from County Down in Ireland. In 1740, he was deeded land from Farnival Green on the North River in Beaufort. In the 1760s, he married Jane Chew Parker, who had come from Maryland with her father and brother. They had one son, William Jr.

Early records of the town indicate that William Thomson owned lot 6 in Old Town, located on Taylor's Creek at the southeast corner of Queen Street. In 1766, the court ordered that a new prison bounds be laid out beginning at the high water mark on the east side of William's wharf, and Thomson was one of the three men appointed to lay out these bounds. In 1767, the court agreed to pay him to buy tar and have the courthouse and prison tarred.

In 1771, Thomson was the naval deputy for the port of Beaufort as well as the commander of two companies of militia during the Regulators' uprising. In 1773, he drew up and signed a petition to Governor Josiah Martin requesting that Beaufort be allowed to send a representative to the general assembly. The governor, angry at Thomson, reportedly wrote to the Earl of Hillsborough that "I can only discover that the deputy naval officer has been guilty of remissness towards me, as well as of error with respect to the Spanish vessel and people." He also stated that Thomson's general character defended him from suspicion of fraud or ill design and that he was not arraigned by any of his neighbors who, as the governor said, "looked upon him invidiously and would not lose an opportunity of doing him injury."

In June of 1774, the court chose Thomson with two others to form a commission for carrying out repairs on the courthouse. The September court minutes, however, say that those mentioned in June were appointed for repairing and "moving the court house where they thought proper."

In August of that year, Thomson served as a delegate to the first provincial congress in New Bern and took part in passing resolutions. He brought word back to the county that after January 1, 1775 no British or East India goods except medicines would be imported into the colony. The people of North Carolina were also told to cease the exportation of tobacco, tar, pitch, and turpentine, and that tea from East India would not be used in their homes.

The second provincial congress was held in New Bern on April 3, 1775 with Thomson again as a delegate. It was this congress that authorized the creation of a committee of safety for each county, town, and military district. Thomson also went as a representative to the third provincial congress in Hillsborough

The 1796 courthouse. (Photo by Diane Hardy.)

on August 20, 1775. To fulfill the authorized formation of regiments for the continental line and minute men, four men from Carteret including William Thomson, commissioned as a colonel, were appointed field officers for companies of 50 men.

On February 21, 1776, Colonel Thomson was appointed to a committee of safety for the New Bern district to enforce the agreement of non-importation and non-exportation. By April, a committee of safety was active in Beaufort.

Thomson and two others represented Carteret County at the fourth provincial congress in Halifax on April 23, 1776. He was appointed one of the commissioners to establish salt works. Thomson was also appointed to a committee to look over the letter from the Beaufort committee, who were concerned about having enough military force to keep enemies from landing and supplying themselves, not to mention committing "hostilities and depredations." Thomson also served on another committee to study the defense and state of the seacoast, as well as a committee to draw up instructions for recruiting officers.

An act was passed on April 23, 1778 for fortifying Cape Lookout Bay, and Thomson was appointed a commissioner of the fortifications. He was instructed to put the bay in a state of defense as soon as possible. The new fort was known as Fort Hancock, and it lasted only two years. In 1779, the governor considered granting a warrant to Thomson for £300 to procure a boat for the fort.

In 1782, Thomson's wife carried a message from the commander of the British fleet who had invaded Beaufort on April 3 to the colonel of the Beaufort militia encamped near the town bridge. Also in 1782, Thomson was treasurer of the town of Beaufort. By 1784, he owned four lots in town valued at £400 and 800 acres of land in the Beaufort district.

In March 1785, Thomson was appointed county trustee and was to call to account the clerk and former trustee to account for what monies were in their hands. He was also to get the money and apply it to the repair of the courthouse and jail, and build a pair of stocks.

During 1796, Thomson served as a justice on the bench and was also treasurer of public buildings in Beaufort and county treasurer. In November, he loaned the commissioners £100 to build the courthouse from money given by the public to build a jail.

He was still on the bench in 1797, and as treasurer for public buildings reported that the jail needed considerable repairs. He later served as administrator, commissioner, and sheriff. Colonel Thomson remained on the bench in 1799. For more than 30 years, he had served the citizens of the town of Beaufort and the county faithfully and to the fullest. When he died in 1803 his first request was that he be carried to his grave by four of his oldest slaves for whom he had ordered new suits of gray trimmed in black.

Among other bequests, Thomson gave 100 acres on the North River to an orphan girl named Jane Simpson, and £10 to each of his stepdaughters to buy gowns. He also ordered his executors to take £20 out of his estate and choose four of the poorest boys in the town of Beaufort and lay it out for their schooling.

WARD

The Ward family dates to 1618 when Captain John Ward arrived at Jamestown Colony. He was elected a burgess from Ward's plantation in Virginia and was the father of Seth Ward, who had a son named Richard. Richard Ward married and had four children, including one son named Edward who married Elizabeth Elam and apparently left Virginia in 1709.

An undated petition from before 1712 for the establishment of a local court at Neuse River in Bath County was signed by Edward Ward, Enoch Ward, and others. Edward was the father of Enoch Ward and Edward Ward Jr., who was originally of Carteret County but later moved to Onslow County and became Colonel Edward Ward in the colonial militia. Edward Jr. was in North Carolina in 1708–1709 and Enoch Ward was in Craven County in 1710. In 1722, at the separation of Carteret Precinct from Craven, Enoch Ward was named a justice. He was also appointed with John Shackelford, John Nelson, Ross Bell, Richard Rustull, and others to the first vestry of St. John's Parish, Beaufort. In 1727, he was a member of the lower house of the North Carolina assembly.

A drawing of a blacksmith, an important tradesman in the early life of a community, by the author.

Enoch Ward was married twice. First to Elizabeth Shackelford, the daughter of John Shackelford, and then to Mary Shackelford Wade, Elizabeth's sister and the widow of Robert Wade. Enoch and Mary's son Enoch Ward Jr. married Abigail Shepard, the daughter of David Shepard. They had seven children.

WICKER

Joseph Wicker and his wife, Ruth, came to Carolina from England in 1666 with a land grant from King James II. By 1706, he was serving as clerk of the court of common pleas and quarter sessions in Currituck Precinct. In 1708, he represented Perquimans Precinct as a member of the house of burgesses. In 1715, he was again clerk of the court of common pleas and quarter sessions in Currituck Precinct, and he held the same office from 1723 to 1747 in Carteret County. His records, in his own hand, are now in Raleigh and are considered the oldest in the county.

Wicker purchased an island in Jarretts Bay, Core Sound, in 1724, where he made his home. It is known today as Davis Island. In 1741, he deeded the island to his daughter Mary for her natural life and then to her son at her death.

In 1727, Wicker was listed as a justice, and in March of 1728, as a warden of St. John's Parish, he was ordered to pay William Davis for construction of the new courthouse. Wicker and Davis had been local officials together in the Albemarle region and Davis was married to Wicker's daughter Mary. James Shackelford also married one of Wicker's daughters. In 1733, Wicker was a representative of the precinct at Edenton. He died in 1742.

WILLIAMS

Robert Williams was born in Ruthin, North Wales on April 29, 1723. He died September 4, 1790 at his home, Dinnant, and was buried 200 yards from the grist mill and dam on the property presently owned by International Paper Company.

In 1763, at the age of 40, Williams sailed from London to New Bern, North Carolina where he was a merchant. In 1765, he purchased two parcels of 75 acres along Taylor's Creek called "Taylor's Old Field" and the white house, plus the western part of the land formerly belonging to James Winwright. Williams also built a salt works on 10 acres on the east end of Front Street, which is listed today as the Davis property but still appears on tax lists as a salt works more than 200 years later.

In June of 1766, Williams went before the court to exhibit his power of attorney from London, perhaps related to a line of credit received from backers in London. In 1767, he returned to England, where he married Elizabeth Dearman. When they returned to Carteret County, a friend of Elizabeth's, Anne Shoebridge, who was 19 at the time, came with them.

On their return, Robert purchased property in New Bern and opened a "Ready Money Store." He also purchased 2 acres in Beaufort from John Pinder on Taylor's Creek east of Stansbury's Gut, and he opened a store in Beaufort as well.

In 1769, Williams began purchasing property along Black Creek between a settlement that would become known as Newport and the mill creek home and mill of William Borden, known today as Mill Creek. Williams dammed the creek and created a large mill pond. Water power was used to operate a saw mill and grist mill. He also raised rice and built the first brick house in Carteret County, using bricks and ballast stone from England.

On November 9, 1770, Williams purchased from Sheriff Chadwick half of Cart (Carrot) Island and 125 acres on the east side of North River that were originally owned by James Shackelford. On February 6, 1771, he made an agreement with Henry Stanton regarding 1 acre of land on the west side of Black Creek containing a saw mill and a grist mill. Stanton was to keep the mills running and pay Williams a portion of the tolls as well as keep a record book.

On May 11, 1771, Thomas Jessop sued Williams for £3,200, to be paid by £1,600 plus interest and debts at court in November. Sheriff Thomas Chadwick seized Williams's lands and property, including the saw mill on the east side of Black Creek; one-half or one-third of the tolls on the grist mill on the same dam; 600 acres of land on the east side of Black Creek that he had bought in 100-acre lots from John Sanders, Joseph Jessop, and Stephen Yates; plus 500 acres on both sides of Little Deep Creek that he had purchased from Joseph and Edward Canaday.

A writ on November 11, 1771 commanded the sheriff to sell the above property. On May 9, 1772, after giving proper notice, the properties were exposed to public vendue and sold. Williams bought back the sawmill, the tolls on the grist mill on the same dam, 600 acres on the east side of Black Creek, and 500 acres on

The Black Creek mill pond. (Photo by Diane Hardy.)

both sides of Little Deep Creek, with all cattle, goods, and chattel. He paid £370 proclamation money, as he was the highest bidder offering the greatest sum.

Williams's wife, Elizabeth, died in 1773, six years after her marriage. They had one son, Richard, who was born on November 28, 1770.

Following the death of Elizabeth, Williams was thrown out of the Core Sound Quaker meeting, being charged with living with and fathering a child by his wife's servant girl, who was married to another man. He later made peace with the brethren and married Anne Shoebridge, his first wife's friend. At this time Robert was 50 and Anne was 25. They had eight children, with three surviving to adulthood.

Richard Williams, the son of Robert and Elizabeth, was married twice. His second marriage in 1796 was to Sarah Stanton, the daughter of Benjamin Stanton.

After overextending himself with so many enterprises, Robert Williams lost his house and the store in New Bern by 1773. Yet even while he was in such distress, he was still purchasing properties. In 1775, he purchased 640 acres on the north side of Newport River from Robert Townshend Dade and his wife, Elizabeth. The property included houses, outhouses, edifices, barns, buildings, gardens, orchards, woods and underwoods, timber trees and trees likely to make timber, and all ways and water courses. The price was £60.

Also in 1775, Williams purchased from William Yates, a planter, 150 acres on the north side of the Newport River near the north branch of Black Creek swamp by Parkers corner and near Colonel Lovick's corner. This property had been granted to Amos Small on May 25, 1757. Small had sold it to Tolson and Tolson to Yates.

On April 23, 1776, Williams was appointed by the provincial congress at Halifax to produce salt. The land at Gallants Point was purchased, and has been used for a variety of businesses since.

In 1777, the property Williams had purchased in 1765 in the town of Beaufort, known today as the Hammock House, was sold as a result of bankruptcy. It was purchased by Benjamin Stanton and was the location of the salt works, which were very important to the area since in April of 1775, the British cut off all supplies to America, including salt.

7. THE NINETEENTH CENTURY

By 1807, Europe was at war and British vessels were waylaying American ships and removing sailors. In 1808, the Embargo Act was in force, with no vessels to be cleared for foreign ports. Commerce ceased in the South and salt making was renewed. Congress had authorized the president to call for detachments of 100,000 militia. North Carolina's quota was 8,071.

Jacob Henry, a Hebrew, was elected to the North Carolina House of Representatives from Carteret County in 1808. When he was reelected in 1809, a disgruntled opponent objected to his qualifying under the constitution. Henry addressed the house with religious tolerance as his subject, but stressed the legal proposition that the provision of the constitution was not applicable to the representatives. The right of the constituency to choose their own representatives was not to be abridged. His speech was so eloquent that it was used for many years in books on elocution.

Also in 1809 the Embargo Act was changed to "nonintercourse" with Great Britain and France, the two countries causing the most trouble. The embargo didn't apply to domestic commerce.

In January 1812, it was noted in a New Bern newspaper that one commercial vessel had arrived from New York, one from Charleston, and two from Beaufort. By February, preparation for war was underway, and it was finally declared on June 19. Meanwhile in December of 1811, there was a violent earthquake near Charleston, and New Bern was shaken for two minutes. On February 7, 1812, tremors were felt at 4:00 a.m. and again at 11:00 p.m.

In May, 1813, a rumor was running around New Bern that Beaufort was blockaded by two British schooners. The local newspaper stated that several vessels whose destination was the Chesapeake Bay had come in to Ocracoke or Beaufort and sent their cargoes to Norfolk through the canal. Beaufort was protected by the fort, and Ocracoke had shoal water, a revenue cutter, and militia.

A schooner arrived off Ocracoke on May 21 and attempted to surprise the cutter. It failed. On June 1, a British armed schooner was seen off the bar of Beaufort, and Captain Otway Burns of Beaufort and his crew sailed for Beaufort on the *Snap Dragon*. The people along the coast had lived with the possibility of attack for four months, and on July 12, a fleet of nine ships including two brigs

A drawing of the Cape Lookout light, by the author.

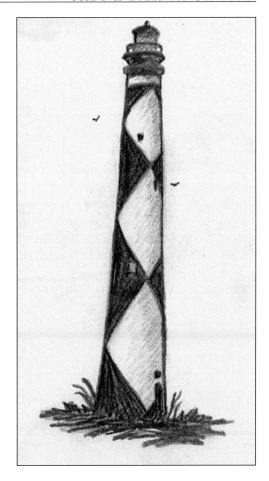

and two schooners anchored off the Ocracoke bar. Nineteen barges, each with an 18-pounder carronade and 40 men, came inside the bar. The British hoped to seize all the vessels and continue on to surprise and capture New Bern.

The surprise was taken away, however, because the revenue cutter managed to escape and warn New Bern. Preparations were quickly made for battle, with women and children evacuated, heavy cannon mounted, breastworks erected, and ammunition supplied from the county and towns of Washington and Beaufort. Militia from surrounding counties came in droves and were ready for the invasion that never took place.

When Raleigh heard of the incident, the governor appointed General Calvin Jones as commander of the seacoast. On his arrival in New Bern, Jones was afraid Beaufort might be attacked and he sent a large detachment to garrison the forts there, including Hampton, Gaston, and Pigott. Although the pending invasion passed and the British fleet sailed south, they sent notice to Ocracoke that the entire coast was blockaded. Apparently this was merely a threat made by the British admiral however, as the fleet sailed away.

AFTER THE WAR OF 1812

In 1820, yellow fever was in Wilmington; there was insurrection among African Americans in Bladen, Onslow, Carteret, and Jones Counties; and the militia was once again called out. In 1821, new members of the assembly included John M. Morehead, who would later become governor and have the city across the Newport River named for him, and Otway Burns, the former captain of the *Snap Dragon*.

By 1827, the railroad was making an impact and a line was proposed between New Bern and Raleigh. Farmers along the line could put their produce on the railway and send it to New Bern, where it would be transferred to barges and taken through the canal to Beaufort and then be shipped overseas.

The Core Creek Canal, as it is known today, was more than 40 years in the making. In 1766, Charles Cogdell represented Carteret County in the assembly, where he introduced and obtained approval legislation to have a canal built that would connect the Clubfoot and Harlowe Creeks. In the early 1800s, the canal had finally been completed, connecting the waters of the Core Sound, the Newport River, the Neuse River, the Pamlico Sound, and Albemarle Sound to the port of Beaufort.

An early aerial view of Fort Macon. (Courtesy Beaufort Historical Association.)

A drawing of the Atlantic Hotel, by the author.

In the late 1820s, the construction of Fort Macon was begun, using brick made in the area. A number of brick masons from other parts of the country arrived to help with the project. The fort was named for Nathaniel Macon who served in congress, was speaker of the house, a senator, president pro tem, and a hunter. At the same time the fort was being built, some of the brick masons worked in Beaufort in the evenings to build a new brick jail and the Masonic Lodge that still stands as the Odd Fellows Lodge in the second block of Turner Street.

During the 1850s, a new taller brick lighthouse was built next to the original one that had been built earlier in the century at Cape Lookout. During the War between the States, both lighthouses were attacked, the older one being destroyed, but the second one stands today in the same location where it was built.

A new steam sawmill, located on the lot overlooking Gallants Channel, was up and running in Beaufort in 1851, making it easier to get lumber for building houses and public places. People were settling in, buying lots, building houses, raising families, and living at the coast. Even those who did not build here, visited.

In 1854, the Atlantic Hotel, located on the water of Taylor's Creek between Pollock and Marsh Streets, was purchased by an entrepreneur from Tarboro who would become involved in the upcoming war. The huge, three-story structure extended out over the water, and a boardwalk connected the hotel with the busy shops and fish houses that lined the waterfront from Turner to Queen Streets.

Church buildings were also going up. In 1854, the new Ann Street Methodist church was built on the lot at the corner of Ann and Craven Streets. Already on the corner of Craven and Broad Streets was the old Methodist church, which was given to the black members of the congregation and today is known as Purvis Chapel, the oldest standing church building in Beaufort. A new Baptist church building was constructed on a lot between Craven and Turner Streets on Ann Street. These three churches were on three corners of the Old Burying Ground. In the 200 block of Ann Street was built the Episcopal church, St. Paul's.

Schools were held in homes during the mid-nineteenth century. One was formed by the Reverend Van Antwerp, rector of St. Paul's in 1858. A schoolhouse large enough for 80 students was erected behind the church building. During the war years, the rector served as the federal chaplain at Fort Macon in addition to rector of St. Paul's Church, Beaufort. The school carried on through these years, but was unable to continue when Van Antwerp left. Thirty years later, St. Paul's School was resurrected.

Other schools included the Beaufort Female Seminary, with Mr. and Mrs. S.D. Pool as principals; the Beaufort Female Institute, with the Reverend William J. Langdon as principal; and the Beaufort Male Academy, with Robert W. Chadwick as principal. There was also a second male academy kept by a Mr. Sweetzer and a primary school run by Miss Sarah A. Davis. S.D. Pool also held a night school for young men whose daily work prevented them from attending day school.

A 1936 photo of St. Paul's Episcopal Church, built c. 1855. (Courtesy Beaufort Historical Association.)

The AME Zion Church Purvis Chapel, built c. 1820. (Photo by Diane Hardy.)

THE WAR BETWEEN THE STATES

As most people know, the Civil War took place in the 1860s. Beaufort and the other coastal communities were not immune from wartime activities. Along the coast, preparations were made by erecting batteries, mounting guns, getting ammunition, and preparing for battle. The Fort Macon battery was commanded by Captain Guion, and Colonel C.C. Tew had been in command of the fort until June 1 when Major De Rosset became the commander. The fort had been strengthened physically but supplies were deficient and there was no skilled ordnance officer.

On May 20, 1861, North Carolina dissolved the union between itself and the other states of the United States of America. It became a free and independent state, and on June 6 adopted the constitution of the Confederate States of America. The governor, in preparation for war, had purchased two small steamers and chartered another to put a small fleet in operation along the coast.

Beaufort's inhabitants in early 1861 had mixed feelings about secession and the possible war. The day before the governor seized all federal institutions, including Fort Macon, following the bombardment of Fort Sumter in South Carolina on

A drawing of Federal Brigadier General Ambrose E. Burnside, by the author.

April 12, a group of local citizens formed the Beaufort Harbor Guards. The group, led by Captain Josiah Pender, crossed the harbor and took over Fort Macon, removing the only person there, Ordnance Sergeant William Alexander of the United States Army.

In the fall of 1861, the Federal government realized the importance of blockading all Southern ports and rivers to prevent the importing of supplies and arms. One of the first targets of Brigadier General Ambrose E. Burnside was Beaufort and its deep-water harbor. Not only could he resupply his troops, but the port made an ideal safe haven from storms and provided a coaling and repair station for the Federal navy. It was in early 1862 that the Federal fleet began the invasion of the coastal waters of North Carolina.

At the same time, the Federal army was advancing following a skirmish in New Bern. Brigadier General John G. Parke, commander of one of Burnside's regiments, was in charge of the capture of Fort Macon, Morehead City, and Beaufort. He requested of two of Beaufort's town authorities, James Rumley and Robert W. Chadwick, that the town stop communicating with the fort. Upon receiving a negative answer, Parke instructed Major John A. Allen with two companies from the 4th Rhode Island to cross from Morehead City and take over the town of Beaufort.

Some time around midnight, the Federals were being ferried through the marshes and around the small islands, and they landed in Beaufort about 2:00 a.m. The troops moved silently through town and set up guards over the wharves and a line of pickets at the rear of town. Thus, when the residents of Beaufort awoke on the morning of March 26, the town was occupied by Federal troops. Some people had fled before the invasion, but those who were loyal to the Union remained and welcomed the troops. The citizens who supported the Confederacy were fearful and remained locked in their homes and businesses.

The Federal troops remained in Beaufort throughout the rest of the war and for 12 years following the official surrender. During that time, they took over many of the fine old houses as command posts, and one in particular is listed as Burnside's headquarters. The Atlantic Hotel became the Hammond Hospital where wounded and sick soldiers were cared for by the Sisters of Mercy. In January 1865, the hospital was broken up and patients were transferred to Mansfield Hospital in Morehead City.

During 1863 the Union occupation of the town gave it a status of safe haven for freedmen or refugee slaves. A camp was established on the north side of town covering the area from Broad, Cedar, Turner, and Live Oak Streets to the Town

A drawing of Federal Brigadier General John Grubb Parke, by the author.

The Washburn Seminary workshop building. (Photo by Diane Hardy.)

Creek. By 1865, this was the Union's second-largest refugee camp in North Carolina and was known as "Union Town." The camp provided instruction in trades as well as schooling, with most blacks attending at night.

Although the war was officially over in April 1865, Federal troops remained in Beaufort essentially running the government until 1877, when the general assembly of North Carolina enacted that the town of Beaufort and County of Carteret be incorporated into a body politic, subject to the laws of North Carolina and the United States. An election was held and Beaufort began its rehabilitation.

AFTER THE CIVIL WAR

The life of Beaufort returned to a semblance of normalcy even though the federal government was more or less controlling local government. One of the good things that happened in several places was the work of the American Missionary Association, established in 1846 by the Congregational Church. The organization determined to build schools or seminaries in the South for the education and training of the freed slaves.

Beaufort was one of the locations. In March of 1866, a part lot was purchased along Cedar Street in the center of the block between Craven and Pollock Streets. The following January the property was sold to the American Missionary Association of New York. By March 1867, the Washburn Male and Female Seminary of Beaufort, North Carolina was incorporated.

The school building was large, with two stories, and was painted brown with dark brown trim. Across the back was the auditorium or chapel. African-American children were gathered from all areas of the county to attend and were boarded in the homes of many people in town during the week, returning home on the weekend.

On the other half of the lot was built St. Stephen's Congregational Church, at the southeast corner of Craven and Cedar Street. This building and its congregation continue on that location to this day. Unfortunately, the seminary building was removed.

In 1895, the seminary trustees purchased the adjacent lot at the southwest corner of Pollock and Cedar Streets. A building was erected to supplement the seminary by providing instruction in the trades of cabinet making, carpentry, and blacksmithing. The success of this part of the school is made obvious by the number of African Americans listed early in the twentieth century applying the trades they were taught.

To assist with the school, a ten-room teacherage was built at the corner of Pollock and Broad Streets and was described as a handsome, two-story house painted yellow with white trim.

Teachers, originally white, came from New York, Connecticut, Michigan, and Ohio. By 1910, black teachers were living in the teacherage, as well, one from Alabama and two from Georgia.

St. Stephen's Congregational Church. (Photo by Diane Hardy.)

The seminary and its associated buildings were given to the local school district in 1917, and by 1965, the property and training center were deeded to St. Stephen's Congregational Church.

By 1885, the Johns Hopkins University Chesapeake Zoological Laboratory was operating in Beaufort at what is known today as the Gibbs House, on the corner of Front and Live Oak Streets. George Bowman Haldeman, a graduate student who was spending summers at the facility, wrote letters to his mother, Anna Haldeman Addams, about the area.

According to Mary Lynn Bryan of Duke University, George Bowman Haldeman was born in 1861 and was Jane Addams's stepbrother. Addams, born in 1860, was the leader of the American settlement house movement in the late 1890s and early 1900s. She founded Hull House in Chicago and was the first American woman to receive the Nobel Peace Prize in 1931.

The descriptions Haldeman wrote are very scientific in nature as he was studying to be a marine biologist. Occasionally, however, there is a mention of something other than his studies, including one note on August 26, 1885 in which he discusses traveling on the *Americus* to Baltimore in September. He says that "At present the

The Gibbs house, built c. 1851. This building was used as the marine laboratory of Johns Hopkins University Chesapeake Zoological Laboratory. (Courtesy Beaufort Historical Association.)

Americus is high and dry on the strand as a result of a fearful storm last Monday night which raged along the southern Atlantic coast and unroofed many houses in Charleston. It began in the afternoon about four o'clock and grew worse until about ten when the fury of the wind and tide was something fearful." According to George, shutters slammed violently, glass broke in windows, and the tide came higher and higher, "dashing against the small breakwater in front of the house and sending a deluge of spray into the yard." Small ships and a larger schooner were stranded and trees were withered. The next morning all was calm.

In another letter on April 22, 1886, he states that "The day is beautiful pale blue tints on the water and soft fluffy clouds" and that "the world moves slower here." And further, "The cows hover round us here as of old with their hungry eyes . . . I never use milk here without realizing what an effort it is for a Beaufort cow to give two or three quarts a day."

His letters continue, with delightful images of what Beaufort was like in the summers in 1885 and 1886, including the people who visited the area, the hotel where they stayed, the food they ate, and what they did for relaxation.

THE FAMILIES AND CONTINUING DEVELOPERS

There were many prominent persons who gave loyalty and service to the town of Beaufort in the nineteenth century and whose families continue to do so today. Some of their stories tell the continuing tale of the development of the town.

ALEXANDER

William Alexander was the ordnance sergeant at Fort Macon when the men of Beaufort took over in 1861. He had been in the army for 30 years and felt he was no longer fit for active service, so he wrote to the chief of ordnance in Washington, D.C. asking what he should do and where he should go. His family was also with him at the fort as was all his personal property. The answer came back to attempt no resistance. He was told to remain in Beaufort.

By 1868, Alexander had purchased part of lot 66 in the first block of Moore Street. He lived there with his wife until his death in 1887 at age 78. The records of St. Paul's Episcopal Church in Beaufort indicate that he was married on October 4, 1860 to Ann L. Livesay of Morehead City. In May of 1861, Ann Letitia Alexander was baptized in the church and she and William were confirmed. Between 1864 and 1881, Ann and William were sponsors and witnesses of several baptisms, and William served as senior warden in 1867.

Alexander is buried in the graveyard of the Episcopal church, and in 1890, his widow sold their property to the church. It remained in the church for several years and was used as the rectory until sold in 1952. Among the residents of the house were Dr. and Mrs. George W. Lay, the rector of St. Paul's from 1918 to 1928. In 1968, the house and property were sold again. The house remains in the same location and is lovingly cared for by its current owners.

The Alexander house, built c. 1852. (Photo by Diane Hardy.)

BELL (A SECOND TIME)

Josiah Fisher Bell, the third child of Josiah and Mary Fisher Bell and the grandson of Malachi and Elizabeth Coale Bell, was married in the 1840s to Susan B. Leecraft. He inherited the house on Turner Street (currently in its original location on the restoration grounds of the Beaufort Historical Association), as well as slaves, two-and-a-half lots in New Town and one-half the North River lands.

At the outbreak of the Civil War, Bell was the collector at Beaufort. He was arrested by General Parke of the Union army when he was trying to get away with 20 $100 Confederate bills that he had received as the duties on the cargoes of the vessels that had run the blockade. There is no record that he was ever incarcerated and it is presumed that he and his family moved out of town to North River.

It is said that Bell was in the Confederate Secret Service, and after learning that the Federals were going to take over the lighthouses at Cape Lookout, he arranged to have troops come from near New Bern, stay at his house, slip over to the lighthouses, blow them up, and return to New Bern.

The old lighthouse was destroyed, but the newer one was merely damaged and still serves today.

OTWAY BURNS

In 1812, Otway Burns of Beaufort was the captain of a merchant ship sailing between New Bern and Portland, Maine. With a sense of patriotism following the recent British threats, he and others, including Colonel Edward Pasteur and William Shepard, arranged to purchase a larger and faster vessel named *Zephyr*, which displaced 147 tons, carried a crew of 75 men, and had 5 carriage guns and 50 muskets. Burns changed the ship's name to *Snap Dragon* and made application for letters of marque, which would allow him to prey on English ships without being considered a pirate.

On *Snap Dragon's* first voyage of six months in 1812–1813, Burns and his crew sailed the Spanish Main and took eight vessels, unloading and burning three, filling three with prisoners, and sending the heavily laden sloop *Fillis*, a prize taken January 18 in the Caribbean, to New Bern.

After a brief respite in Beaufort, *Snap Dragon* set out on its most rewarding voyage on June 3, 1813. Burns sailed from Newfoundland to South America, capturing several British ships including two barks, five brigs, and three schooners with a total value of $1 million. The third voyage early in 1814 to the Spanish Main was not as successful as the previous trips.

The tomb of Otway Burns.
(Photo by Diane Hardy.)

With Burns laid up and suffering from a debilitating illness, *Snap Dragon* sailed its fourth and final voyage on May 26, 1814 under the command of Captain W.R. Graham. On June 30, the privateer was captured by the British ship *Martin*, not the *Leopard* as some have suggested. *Snap Dragon* was taken to England and her remaining crew put in Dartmoore prison.

Following the war, Burns ran a shipbuilding business on Town Creek in Beaufort where in 1815 he built the first steamboat to work the waters of the Cape Fear River, *Prometheus*. In 1821, he was elected to the North Carolina legislature, serving seven years in the house of commons and five years in the senate.

After three marriages, one son, and the loss of his business, properties, and friends, Burns was appointed by President Andrew Jackson as keeper of the lighthouse on Portsmouth Island near Ocracoke, where he lived out the rest of his life. At his death, his body was placed in a shallow-bottom centerboard sailboat designed for Carteret County waters, covered with a piece of jib sail, and brought to Beaufort for burial in the Old Burying Ground on Ann Street.

DAVIS

There apparently were other Davises who came to Carteret County. One in particular was a prolific builder of houses, most of which stand today. James Davis, born in 1781, was married in 1803 to Elizabeth Adams who had been born in 1783, the daughter of a farmer living in Core Creek.

The William J. Potter house, built c. 1832. (Photo by Diane Hardy.)

A drawing of the James Davis house, built c. 1817, by the author.

In 1817, James built a house at the northeast corner of Moore and Ann Streets where he and Elizabeth raised their family. James worked at Fort Macon as a brick mason while it was being built at the eastern end of Bogue Banks across from the Beaufort harbor.

In 1829, he built a new house in the second block of Moore Street. The beauty of this house is that it is two-and-a-half stories tall with the first floor high off the ground, allowing room for the basement workshop where he spent time building cabinets and furniture.

While at Fort Macon, James met William Jackson Potter who married Elizabeth Harris Davis, the daughter of James and Elizabeth Adams Davis. They moved with her parents to the new house until after the birth of the Potters' first child. In 1830, James deeded the east end of lot 66 on the southeast corner of Ann and Moore Streets to his daughter. The deed included the premises, which apparently became the home of the Potters. When Potter purchased a lot on Ann Street in the New Town, his father-in-law also built the couple's new house.

Davis's houses were generally built in the popular Bahamian style, with double front porches on two-and-a-half stories. His floor plans rarely varied, for each of the houses in Beaufort with which he was connected had a side hall and two rooms opening from the hall on each floor. He used materials native to North

Carolina and, for safety's sake, built a kitchen separated from the main house, perhaps with a dog run or porch joining them.

DUNCAN

Although the family's history begins in the eighteenth century, the primary activity of the Duncans took place in the nineteenth century and continues to this day with the many descendants still living in the area. According to family histories, the first Duncan in Beaufort was John. The early court minutes indicate that in 1730 a John Duncan (who could have also been Dunean or Duman, for it is difficult to read some of the early writing), age 4, was to be bound to William Owen until he was 21 to learn "the art and mistery" of a "taylor."

The next entry is in 1769 when Thomas and Susanna Duncan sold lot 15 in Beaufort and the next year purchased lot 33. Then, in 1772, Thomas Duncan sold lot 33 to William Borden. Captain Thomas Duncan, born in 1769, was married and had a son also named Thomas (1806–1880).

The Carteret Academy, built c. 1854. (Photo by Diane Hardy.)

The Duncan house, built c. 1790. (Photo by Diane Hardy.)

Records indicate that the property that was purchased by Captain Duncan was originally owned by Edward Fuller, who most likely built a part of the house that can be seen today. Following Fuller's death in 1790, the lot and house became the property of William Dennis Jr. who willed it to his brother-in-law Nathan Adams in 1802. Adams's daughter and son-in-law James Davis sold the property to Benjamin Tucker Howland in 1820, when it finally came into the hands of the Duncan family.

The house was built in the style of those of the Bahamas, with double porches, turned columns, and three chimneys. The original house was half the size that it is today.

Thomas Duncan added the west end, presumably as a ship's chandlery dealing in turpentine, molasses, rope, and other commodities, although with the growth of his family it is possible he and Elisha merely needed more living space.

William B. Duncan was born in 1836 and married two times, first to Sally Ramsey, the daughter of Isaac and Charity F. Ramsey. Sally died in 1867 at age 21 and their son Thomas L. Duncan married Laura Nelson. Thomas and Laura had a daughter named Lena who lived in the family house on lot 12 in Old Town, known as the Carteret Academy.

Miss Lena was a well-beloved teacher who is remembered even to this day by her former students.

Following Sally's death, William B. Duncan married Emily Frances Jones. Their son David J. Duncan married Fanny Dudley in 1898, and the couple had two children, David Dudley Duncan and Emily Frances Duncan. At their father's death, their uncle Julius "Jule" Fletcher Duncan married their mother. Many of the Duncans' descendants live in Beaufort today.

MANNEY

James Lente Manney Jr. was born in 1827, the son of Dr. James L. Manney who came to Beaufort in the early 1800s. Dr. Manney was a partner in the building of the canal that connects Beaufort with the Neuse River. His son went to medical school in the 1840s, returning before 1860 with his doctor's certificate. In 1848, he was married to Julia Ann Fulford, whose father was the lighthouse keeper at Cape Lookout.

James L. Manney Jr. enlisted in the Beaufort Harbor Guards in 1861 and was at Fort Macon when it was captured in 1862 by Federal forces. During the remainder of the war he and his unit helped build pontoon bridges and boats in Kinston and Goldsboro as well as in Virginia. He was released from the service in 1865 and, following the death of his first wife, married Sidney Styron in 1867. He continued to practice medicine in Beaufort until his death in the late 1800s.

There is an interesting, though sad story about Dr. Manney Sr.'s daughter Nancy L. Manney, who was born about 1820, the oldest child of Dr. and Mrs. Manney. Charles Grafton Wilberton French from Berkley, Massachusetts came to Beaufort as a tutor and met Nancy Manney through her father. Nancy and Charles fell in love, but their romance was discouraged by Dr. Manney, who wanted Nancy to stay home and care for her seven younger siblings.

Eventually French told Nancy that he was going to seek his fortune elsewhere and that when he could, he would send for her and they would be married. In 1844, he left Beaufort for the west. In 1851, he was in California where he studied law, and in 1854, he moved to Sacramento and practiced until 1875. He married a widow and became active in the community.

In 1875, he rose in his profession, being appointed by President Grant to be chief justice of the supreme court in the territory of Arizona. It is presumed that he moved to Prescott, Arizona at this time. In 1880, he was reappointed to a second term as chief justice.

Over the years he had written to Nancy, but his letters were intercepted by the Beaufort postmaster, who confessed before he died that he had given them to her father. Nancy thus had no way of contacting him and thought that he had forgotten about her.

In 1885, after French's wife died, he decided to write directly to the postmaster asking about Nancy. One story says the postmaster turned the letter over to Nancy and that she herself answered French's letter. Another says that the postmaster wired Charles and told him to come to Beaufort by the fastest possible way, since Nancy was dying of the "galloping consumption."

A drawing of James Lente Manney Jr., by the author.

When Charles received this information in whatever form it took, he returned to Beaufort, and on May 20, 1886, Nancy L. Manney married her beloved Charles Grafton Wilberton French. Within a month, on June 14, 1886, Nancy succumbed to her consumption and died in the arms of her husband. She is buried in the family plot in the Old Burying Ground on Ann Street. Charles died in San Francisco in 1891.

PENDER

Josiah Pender was born to wealth. In 1835, he received an appointment to West Point but left after seven months because he didn't like the discipline. He still, however, pictured himself as a dashing military officer. He served in the Mexican War in 1846 where he was dishonorably discharged for insubordination. Although he appealed the discharge, he was given administrative duties and resigned after five months.

A drawing of Stephen Decatur Pool, by the author.

From 1848 to 1860, Pender pursued an artistic career and built a prosperous jewelry business in Tarboro. This expanded into a shipping business when he purchased three steamships operating between Beaufort, Bermuda, and New York. In 1856, Pender purchased the Atlantic Hotel in Beaufort and moved his family from Tarboro and into the hotel.

When secession was the talk of the town, Pender used his own funds to recruit and outfit his own militia unit. On April 14, 1861, without orders, his Beaufort Harbor Guards took control of Fort Macon.

Pender was active in the building-up of troops at the fort, but in November his wife was ill, barracks life was dull, and he requested leave, which was denied. He decided to go home anyway, was court-martialled, and convicted of being absent without leave and making false statements to the commandant at Fort Macon. He was dismissed from state service and the Confederate army in December.

In 1862, he used his steamships as blockade runners. By October 1864, he had contracted yellow fever, died at age 45, and was buried in the Old Burying Ground in Beaufort.

POOL

Stephen Decatur Pool was a printer in New Bern before coming to Beaufort, and in 1854, he started a local newspaper. Local history says that Pool was hired by Malachi Roberson as a tutor for his daughters and later headed the Ladies Seminary in the home that today is known as the Masonic Lodge on Turner Street. Pool and his wife, Caroline Sydney Lockwood Pool, had 14 children, three of whom died in their youth. Their oldest, James Harrell Pool, was the only one to remain in Beaufort.

Stephen D. Pool enlisted in the Confederate army during the Civil War. Following the surrender of Fort Macon, he was paroled and sent home. In 1864, he was a lieutenant colonel and chief of artillery stationed in Goldsboro. By 1865, he was listed as a commanding officer stationed in Tarboro.

While living in Beaufort, Stephen and his family attended St. Paul's Episcopal Church where Mrs. Pool played the organ. In 1872, he served as clerk to the general assembly in Raleigh. He published a magazine in Raleigh in 1874, and was nominated for superintendent of public instruction. He resigned in 1876 and moved his family, with the exception of James Harrell, to New Orleans where he and several of his sons were prominently connected to the *Times Picayune* newspaper.

A drawing of the R. Rustull house, built c. 1732, by the author.

ROBERSON/HOWLAND

Susan Pigott Roberson, born in 1841, was the daughter of Malachi Bell and Sarah Ann Pigott Roberson. She and her sisters are credited with having made the flag that Captain Pender raised at Fort Macon in April 1861.

The family lived on Front Street from 1820 to 1850, when Malachi built a large combination residence and school in the second block of Turner Street, known today as the Masonic Lodge.

Susan and her sisters were tutored by Stephen Decator Pool. The home eventually was the site of the Beaufort Female Seminary.

Susan's sister Cinderilla married James Harrell Pool in 1866, and in 1869 Susan married Levi C. Howland. They had three children. Levi served in the Civil War and afterwards was one of only seven public school teachers in the county. In 1881, he became Carteret County's first superintendent of public schools.

Susan and Levi lived in the old family place, originally on Front Street but turned facing Craven Street. This house today is on the restoration grounds of the Beaufort Historical Association and serves as the Mattie King Davis Art Gallery.

A drawing of Susan Pigott Roberson, by the author.

8. The Twentieth Century

Beaufort continued to grow. The town changed slowly, ploddingly, skeptically, and carefully. There were lulls in which not much happened, but there were also spurts of building and great influxes of people moving to the area. This was no different than the previous centuries. Nothing has changed to this day.

In the early 1900s a few things happened that were very important in the town. St. Paul's Episcopal Church School came to life once again, following a more than 30-year lapse in teaching. In 1906, the railroad came across the causeway and began regular visits to Beaufort. In 1907, the railroad station on Broad Street was built and a new, large brick courthouse was erected on courthouse square. The old one was auctioned off and torn down.

The First World War affected many here in Beaufort, with young men going off to fight in Europe, many leaving the town and county for the first time. Commercial fishing was doing well, with the advent of the menhaden fisheries in both Beaufort and Morehead City. The menhaden is a small, bony, and inedible fish. Known locally as shad, it does make good fertilizer and fish meal food for pigs and chickens. The oil of the fish is used in the manufacture of paint and linoleum.

Also in the twentieth century, the streets of Beaufort slowly began to be fixed up, first with oyster shells crushed by rollers, and eventually with pavement.

Beaufort Published

In the 1930s, a wonderful booklet called "The Old Topsail Inlet: A Story of Old and New Beaufort" was put together by Georgia W. Neal and F.B. Mace. They wrote the following message to their readers: "The mission of this publication is to acquaint you with what is happening this summer in Beaufort, N.C. when you are seeking 'Some Place to Go—Something to Do—Something to See.' " They also stated:

> When you come to Beaufort you may expect to find, besides our historic interests, the following forms of amusement: Swimming in the roaring ocean or the peaceful sound, golf, tennis, fishing for deep sea fish such

An early class picture at the St. Paul's Episcopal Church School. (Courtesy Beaufort Historical Association.)

as dolphin, marlin, and amberjack or fishing in nearby waters abundant with trout and other less spirited fish, hunting for deer, geese, duck, and quail, skeet shooting, soft ball, sun bathing, aquaplaning, surfboard riding, bowling, movies, many social activities, dancing, sailing, motor boating, and horseback riding. What other resort boasts more activities?

Included in this booklet was an article by M. Leslie Davis titled "Historic Beaufort," much of which is already addressed in early chapters of this book. However, Davis wrote that Beaufort people have always been interested in education. He talks of James Winwright who left money for a teacher and school in his will. In addition, he mentions William Shepard who was principal of the Beaufort School in 1777, and whose daughter married a Pettigrew and became the mother of General Johnston Pettigrew, a famous member of the Confederate Army.

With regard to Fort Macon, Davis stated that Robert E. Lee visited in November 1840 to inspect the new fort. According to Davis, the cannon on top of the Otway Burns gravestone was the landmark between Old Town and New Town, embedded in the sand at the waterfront and Pollock Street. Today there is an iron marker at the site with information about the distinction between Old Town and New Town.

A short paragraph mentions the Biddle family: Charles of Philadelphia and his wife, Hannah Shepard of Beaufort. Davis writes that "It is supposed that James Biddle was born in Beaufort." Biddle was a noted commodore in the War of 1812 and his brother Charles was president of the U.S. Bank in Philadelphia, which was put out of business by President Johnson in the 1800s.

As mentioned earlier, the Stanton family was important to the growth of Beaufort. Davis mentions that the father of Edwin M. Stanton, secretary of war in President Lincoln's cabinet, was born in Beaufort at the old home that is still owned by the family to this day.

Many other prominent people are mentioned in Neal's booklet, including Manteo, the Native American who sailed to England in 1585. Davis claims Manteo was born on Harker's Island near Beaufort. This is a possibility, but it has not been proven in modern-day research. But Joseph A. Physioc, a famous scenic painter, was from Beaufort, as was the mother of novelist Tristram Tupper, author of *Adventuring*, in which local Beaufortites were characters under fictitious names.

A drawing of the 1907 courthouse, by the author.

Beaufort's Norfolk Southern Railroad depot. (Courtesy Beaufort Historical Association.)

Davis also relates the stories of the courthouses in Beaufort, and talks of Cecil C. Buckman, born in Beaufort on Ann Street, who was prominent in Baltimore as an owner of Buckman Fruit Company, a partner of United Fruit Company. Relatives of Buckman still live in Beaufort.

Some of the photos and drawings show well-known houses that still look much the same today. The back half of the booklet contains advertising from local merchants, including F.R. Bell, Druggist (Bell's Drug Store today); the Beaufort Graded School, operating in these days as Beaufort Elementary School; the Front Street Gulf Station, now known as Finz, a popular eatery; and the Tally-Ho Tavern, which has been changed into a clothing store.

Others included the Beaufort Theatre, touted as the only air-conditioned theatre in Carteret County; the Norfolk, Baltimore, and Carolina Line; direct all-water freight service; the Beaufort Grocery Company, a grocery store that today is a restaurant using the same name; Barbour's Machine Shop, no longer in the same building but still operating; Ye Olde Beaufort Inn, replaced by the BB&T bank building, yet with one section retained and used as apartments; C.D. Jones Co., stating that deliveries were made to Atlantic Beach during the summer (a long way to go on a bicycle); Scarboro-Safrit Lumber Company, today Safrit's Lumber operating in Beaufort and Jacksonville; and the First Citizens Bank & Trust Company.

In the next decade another brochure was prepared entitled "You'll Like Beaufort North Carolina 'By the Sea.' " On the cover, below a photograph of the menhaden fleet at dock on Beaufort's waterfront, were the words "Historic, Picturesque, Hospitable, Growing!"

This booklet gave facts and statistics such as the location, size, elevation, temperature, rainfall, population, and transportation routes to Beaufort. Also mentioned were scientific laboratories, farming, menhaden fisheries, and tourism. The book also stated that "Beaufort is the county seat of Carteret County, and the center of trade for an area representing well over 20,000 people, 84.9 percent of which are native born white."

Under the heading "A Favorite with Tourists," there is a passage that reads, "Each summer a colony of artists from the Woman's College of the University of North Carolina is attracted by the peaceful beauty of the town," and goes on to describe the old houses and other historic areas.

As much as 60 to 70 years ago, Beaufort and its citizenry realized that tourism was a good thing. And it continues so today.

A brochure for "The Old Topsail Inlet." (Courtesy Beaufort Historical Association.)

VOICES OF BEAUFORT

Realizing the serious need to retain the history of the town, the Beaufort Historical Association began audio and video taping interviews with various citizens of age who were willing to share their memories of the Beaufort they knew in the first quarter of the twentieth century. The following are excerpts from several of these interviews.

One of Beaufort's now-departed citizens stated that the Howard Jones Hardware Store made deliveries with an old dray horse that also took children for rides, drove the oil wagon, and the hearse.

At St. Paul's, the children lined up in the back of the school while the band played the "Star-Spangled Banner" and they saluted the flag as it was raised on the flagpole. When the band began playing "The Double Eagle," or some other traditional march, the children would march into the assembly, where they would have prayer and singing, then go to their different classrooms. "Miss" Nannie P. Geoffrey was the head of the school, reportedly a large and mannish-looking woman who dressed in a long, black dress with a high collar and a chain around her waist holding at least 40 or 50 keys.

Nannie P. Geoffrey, headmistress of St. Paul's School. (Courtesy St. Paul's Episcopal Church.)

St. Paul's Episcopal School. (Courtesy Beaufort Historical Association.)

Beaufort Graded School was the next step in education. After school, the girls would go to one of the little corner stores, get a cucumber pickle and a box of crackers, walk to one of the bridges or the shore, and settle in for a time of talk. The boardwalk, located where the Front Street sidewalk is today, ran from the foot of Queen Street in front of the old Inlet Inn and just beyond. Each house along the way had a personal boardwalk that went out into Taylor's Creek from the boardwalk.

Beyond Pollock Street, many houses had their own breakwaters and small docks. Eventually the area behind these breakwaters was filled in by dredging Taylor's Creek, and Front Street was extended. In the summertime, the hotel was full of up-state vacationers with babies abounding, and the boardwalk was full of mothers pushing baby carriages and enjoying the seaside. The children, and adults as well, enjoyed swimming from the old dock at the Inlet Inn.

For entertainment there were movies at the local cinema, shows with Grayden and M.C. Paul performing their wondrous music and stories and, of course, there were dances for young people. Life in Beaufort was good.

The Reverend Donald Crooms was interviewed in 1995 and related stories of his ancestors and their lives in Beaufort. Abel Murrell, his aunt's father, was a slave child, taught to read by his master's daughter Sally Murrell. She would keep her school books and use them to teach Abel. In return, he cared for Sally, making sure she had whatever she needed.

125

Abel married Mary Jane Priscilla Riddick, who was named after her father's three sisters. The family came from the James City area, near New Bern, and settled at North River. Their home was a one-room house, with dirt floors and sheets dividing the space for rooms. Abel and Mary Jane had 13 children.

In the 1890s, there was a North River migration to Mississippi, organized by a Professor Brown, an educated, sharply dressed, and well-groomed man who convinced some of the people they could make a better living and help families at home by moving to Mississippi. The people had no idea who they would work for, they only knew they could send money home to Beaufort to help their families.

The Smith family went, but when one of the aunts wanted to come home, she had to have a friend in Mississippi write letters to someone she had worked for in Beaufort, asking for help. The gentleman sent money for a train ticket and when she returned to Beaufort she followed through on her promise to work for him until she died.

James Smith also put his mother and sister on a train and they came back to Beaufort. He followed by running away, traveling through swamps, marsh, and water, catching rides on carts traveling east, and finally arriving at home. He was later hired by the Work Projects Administration to work as a lead man with crews digging ditches and canals for drainage.

Smith did all right. He bought farm land, built a big two-story house, and helped build the Baptist church where he served as a deacon. He was an undertaker as

A welcoming party in Beaufort's brand-new station waiting for the first train to arrive in the town in 1907. (Courtesy Beaufort Historical Association.)

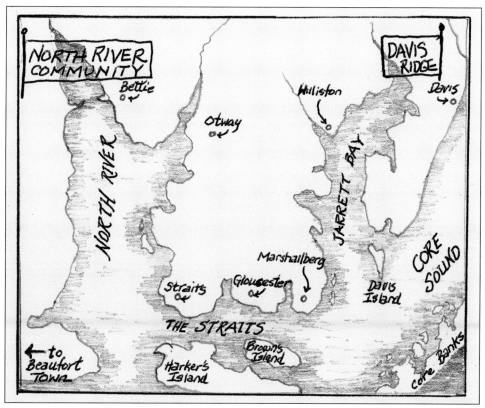

A map showing part of downeast, the North River community, and Davis Ridge, by the author.

well, dressing bodies, putting salt on the lips, and pennies on the eyes to keep the lids from opening. In winter the burials were held the day after the death but the services would be in warmer weather. James's mother, who had been a slave, was the first person in North River to have a funeral.

The first public school appeared in 1893. Abel Murrell's daughter Rachel, who was also Donald Croom's aunt, attended school until she was 19 or 20. School was held for only two to three months, and in the winter, the students had to collect firewood and build a fire in the stove. Teachers from Beaufort, including one man and several women, would come to the community and be housed in the homes of citizens during school sessions. The teachers were very strict but the students remembered what they learned.

In an influenza epidemic in 1918, when Rachel Murrell was 31, she lost her husband, a child, an aunt, and two or three first cousins. She also lost her mother to cancer at the same time. Her husband had ordered her a car, which she didn't really want as she was happy with her horse and buggy. But when her husband died, that was the end of the car.

As there were not a lot of doctors in the area, the people in the North River community used yaupon and other herbs as healing remedies. The women

Louise Nelson's house. (Photo by Diane Hardy.)

primarily did housework and had babies. They took in washing for white families even though there were not many well-to-do white families in the neighborhood.

Some of the North River families were from the region called Davis Ridge. They were more light-skinned than others in the area. The Ridge was at the other end of the island where Davis lived with his slaves. When his slaves learned of their freedom at the end of the Civil War, they went by boat to North River. Davis had refused to let them go, so they left in the middle of the night taking pigs, chickens, and everything else they needed. When Davis woke the next morning, he found his slaves gone. None of his daughters knew how to cook, so the only solution was to go ask the former slaves for help.

In 1933, a great hurricane almost washed everything away, including the fish factory, the church, the school, and all that they had built. The Davises from Davis Ridge were very clever; they learned to make their own meal and their own clothing and sustained their families with no help from others. Following the hurricane, many North River families moved to Beaufort and some became teachers.

Louise Hudgins Nelson's interview is filled with wonderful memories of growing up, getting married, and raising a family all in her hometown of Beaufort. She was born in 1911 and lived in the same house where her parents had lived until her death in March 2002. She saw the arrival in Beaufort of electricity, telephones, the sewer system, paved streets, and plumbing.

Louise Nelson's parents were married in the house, although the wedding had been planned for the church. A neighbor child was sick with typhoid and eventually died, but out of respect for the neighbors, the couple changed their wedding plans to a quiet ceremony. Louise's mother also had typhoid and nurses came from New Bern on the train to take care of her, staying right in the house. Her mother died when she was very young, and Louise was raised by her grandparents. Her father was in the Coast Guard and away much of the time.

Nelson's childhood memories include going to the corner of Ann and Pollock Streets to pump water before her family got a pump on the back porch, and playing in the street under the light in the summertime. According to her, there was one light hanging in the middle of the intersection. Since there were no cars or traffic to speak of, the young people would gather under the light and play hide and seek and other games. The light was powered by a generator.

Before electric lights were installed in the house in 1925, kerosene lamps were used, one upstairs and one downstairs. The lamps were cleaned, polished, and filled daily. Since cooking was not done at night, there was no lamp in the kitchen. In the dining room, the lamp was used for studying on the table. When electricity arrived, the wires were hung on the outside of the house with one strung across to the middle of the room ending with a bulb in a socket. When plumbing arrived, they had one spigot in the kitchen. The bathroom consisted only of a commode, which was put under the stairs where it remains today.

Swimming was another popular activity, but only at high tide. The children would go to the Inlet Inn dock, swim until the tide started out, and then head for home. Nelson said she had to wear an old dress because her grandmother wouldn't let her be seen in a bathing suit. The good swimmers would swim across

Ann Street with its single streetlight. (Courtesy Beaufort Historical Association.)

The flood of 1927, with the Sea Breeze Theatre in the background. (Courtesy Beaufort Historical Association.)

Taylor's Creek to Bird Shoal, where there were only sea oats and sand dunes. You could even see the white caps on the ocean coming across the bar.

On Bird Shoal there was a high wheel for drying nets. The boys were brave and would get in the wheel and go round as it turned, squawking so loud you could hear it all over town. When the menhaden boats were tied up at the town docks, the boys would climb up to the crow's nests and dive straight down into the water.

Floundering at night was another summertime event. To see the flounder, one would put a wire basket on a stick out on the front of a boat, put lightwood in it, and set it on fire. Then, while wading along the shoreline, gig the flounders. The next day the fish were put in a cart and sold for a quarter.

In the summer the train would come in at 11:00 a.m. to the depot on Broad Street. Porters from the Inlet Inn would meet the tourists with their large cart, load the baggage, and all would walk back to the inn. Many of the visitors brought trunks full of clothing as they stayed for one or two months. In the evening, about 7:00 p.m., a second train would come bringing the newspaper from Virginia.

Saturdays were often spent at the picture show. The Sea Breeze theatre, located on Front Street where the North Carolina Maritime Museum is today, showed silent movies. You could get in for a dime, buy a bag of parched peanuts for a nickel, and settle down to watch the show. The owner's daughter Glennie Paul would play the piano, and as the music got faster and faster, going along with the action of the movie, the children would get excited, clap their hands, stomp their feet, and shout until Mr. Paul stopped the movie and warned them he wouldn't finish running the film until they stopped.

Summer was also the time when the photographer would visit. He and his donkey would walk all over town, stopping at each house to take a picture of the children on the donkey.

Front Street was the first in town to be paved, which was a delight for the young people, who skated and rode bicycles all afternoon until dark. There were also small shops on every corner where the children would take a paper sack or an egg and trade it in for a piece of candy.

During the First World War, the train came to the station in Beaufort to pick up the soldiers. Everyone in town would gather there, including Red Cross women in their white scarves. They would give each soldier a cake. The boys would get on the train and lean out the windows to wave goodbye. When the war was over, on November 11, 1918, the train came back to town with the survivors. The church bells rang, whistles blew, and everyone was on their porch waving as the train went by on Broad Street.

Whenever there was a fire, the men would run through town shouting. All the people in the neighborhood would grab a bucket and help put it out. When the

An early horse-drawn steam fire engine. (Courtesy Chief James Lynch, Beaufort Fire Department.)

The Ocean View Cemetery on Ann Street. (Photo by Diane Hardy.)

town finally got a fire station, on Broad Street across from the new courthouse, they also got a fire truck that was pulled by a big, black horse. The horse also pulled the trash cart through town, but when the "wild cat" whistle at the fire station went off, it would leave the trash cart and go directly to the fire station to do its duty.

If there was a death in town, a tall African-American man was hired who went from door to door to let people know who had died. He carried a card with a black border hung from a black ribbon, which he showed to the person who answered the door. On the card was the name of the deceased and the time of the funeral.

School was a real experience in Beaufort. Louise Nelson attended St. Paul's School from kindergarten to the third grade, then moved on to Beaufort Graded School. Kindergarten started at age four and the room was located on the third floor of the school building at St. Paul's on Ann Street. At age five, the children returned to the kindergarten room in the morning. In the afternoon, they went to "chart" class on the first floor. They sat on a bench while the teacher taught them to read from a chart so that they would be able to read when they entered first grade. Many of the teachers were from the North.

There was a service every day in the church and Louise remembered wearing white stockings to school. Her grandmother asked her why she always got the knees dirty. Louise, of course, said they had to kneel to pray! Easter morning at sunrise, the St. Paul's School band, with Miss Nannie Geoffrey leading, would march down Ann Street, stopping at every corner and playing "Christ is Risen."

In the spring, there was a county commencement ceremony with students from all the schools in the county gathering together for races, a May Pole dance, glee club singing, a concert, spelling bees, and marching bands, and it lasted all day. Nelson also remembered wearing long underwear, which didn't come off until Easter Sunday. Then, she says, you wore little white socks and white shoes, and felt naked! It didn't matter if the weather turned cold again, either. And to go barefoot, you had to wait until June 1.

In 1927, the causeway between Beaufort and Morehead City opened. There were not many cars in town, but a neighbor of Nelson's had one. It was loaded with all the folks it could carry and then driven across the bridge to Morehead City. The drawbridge at that time was on the west end of Ann Street with another at the end of the causeway to cross over the water to Morehead City. Before the causeway was built, if you wanted to go to Morehead City you took a ferry that carried two cars, or you took your own boat.

Another event that required a boat or barge was the annual church picnic at Atlantic Beach. Mothers cooked huge picnic lunches of fried chicken, deviled eggs, pies, and cakes, all packed in picnic baskets. They would gather at the dock, load up, and cross over the water to the sound side of the beach where they would unload, the men carrying the baskets, and all walking through the dunes to the pavilion where they would have lunch at noon. After swimming and playing in the ocean, they would return to the barge for the trip back home, sunburned, tired, and happy.

Sunday dinners consisted of chicken, collard greens, and biscuits, sometimes with baked beans cooked on Saturday. No seafood was served on Sundays, and at that time shrimp were not for eating, they were used for bait only. There were no refrigerators or ice boxes, so food was cooked in the daytime with leftovers put in the drawers of the buffet for supper at night. Some cheese and molasses might be added in the evening.

On Sunday afternoons, there was a visit to the cemetery with flowers for Nelson's mother's grave, followed by a trip "out of town" through the town gate located near the present-day elementary school. The gate was used to keep cattle out of town, and today there is a plaque where it was located.

With the coming of ice boxes, in the spring the ice plant would bring a chart to nail on the front porch. A pointer on the chart told the plant whether you needed 10 pounds, 15 pounds, etc. The men would saw the ice at the truck and bring the block in the house with huge tongs, while the children gathered behind the truck to get the shavings to eat.

Thanksgiving and Christmas were holidays to remember. All over town before both holidays you could hear turkeys gobbling but silence would descend as soon as the holiday was nigh. Turkeys were raised outside of town and brought in to a coop in the backyard where they would sound off.

The Ward-Hancock house, built c. 1726. (Photo by Diane Hardy.)

The tree for Christmas was holly, brought in from out in the country. Holly was also used for decoration behind photos and pictures and over curtain rods. The tree was put up on Christmas eve. There were no lights, only small birthday-size candles that clipped on the branches. Ornaments were breakable spun-glass balls on ribbons. The next morning the candles were lit when Santy had come. As soon as everyone caught a glimpse of the tree all lit up, the candles were extinguished.

On Christmas morning, a group of African Americans would celebrate the day by marching through town beating on tin pans and waking everyone up to announce the good news. If there had been a death in the house during the year, there was no tree, only presents and cookies.

The Moores, Louise Nelson's great grandparents, lived on Shackelford Banks where her great grandfather was a whaler. They moved to Beaufort in the 1800s because of the storms. Others on the banks went to Marshallberg and Morehead City. The Moores were "laid back" folks according to Nelson, while her grandmother Chadwick from Straits was very religious. When there were revivals in Beaufort, her great grandmother would sail over wearing a black silk apron and bonnet and take grandmother Chadwick with her.

Every summer on the banks, they would have traptic, or revival meetings. The preacher and others would go over and stay five or six weeks at a time, holding church every night. Nelson's great grandmother Moore would feed the people seafood and garlic. One night at a revival, Moore shouted so much she passed out and was stiff as a board. Some of the men took her home on a stretcher made from a door of the church, but she woke up on the way home.

After the Moores moved to Beaufort, Louise's grandfather opened a store on Front Street. He was the first merchant in town to deliver groceries and canned goods.

In August 1887, there was an earthquake. As Louise states, it was a hot night with the moon shining and the air so still you could hear the voices of people talking all over town. Her grandparents were upstairs with three children when the house began to sway. Her grandfather grabbed a lamp and the children, and struggled down the stairs. People were out in the street screaming and yelling because no one knew what was happening. The earthquake was actually in Charleston, South Carolina, which was destroyed, but the tremors were felt all the way to Beaufort and they kept up until November.

There was a hurricane as well that visited Beaufort in the late 1800s, destroying the old Atlantic Hotel on Front Street. It was a Saturday night and the hotel was full of people dancing, many of whom drowned when the hotel was washed into the water. Another hurricane was predicted in 1933 in Beaufort. There was a tower in John Duncan's yard, and depending on the weather that was on the way, he would raise flags warning the townspeople. One morning the hurricane flag went up and at the same time in another home, the "glass was falling" in a family's barometer. Wind and rain blew in the windows and took the roof off the schoolhouse.

The first train to Beaufort waiting on the causeway. (Courtesy Beaufort Historical Association.)

135

WRITTEN STORIES OF BEAUFORT

In the late 1900s, Nancy D. Russell, a Beaufort native, began writing stories for the local newspaper, the Gam. Some of her memories are reprinted here, with thanks to both Nancy for writing them and the newspaper for printing them.

Nancy's father was the engineer on the first train into Beaufort, and he wrote an article about the early passenger trains for the Carteret Historical Research Association's book *The Heritage of Carteret County* in 1980. One of the interesting facts about the arrival of this massive, smoke-belching machine was that it had to come into Beaufort backward as there was no "wye" on which to turn it around.

The tracks were laid on a trestle over the muck, mud, and marsh that lay between Morehead City and Beaufort. Most of the time the engine pulled passenger cars but in the summer, for the people who had discovered Beaufort from "up north" as well as for travel from Beaufort, the Norfolk & Southern Railway added a Pullman car.

At first, the depot was located just across Gallant's Channel at the point, but within a year or so the station on Broad Street at Pollock was built. Today the train station is used for public hearings and meetings for the town, and a wonderful display of memorabilia from the days of the train in Beaufort has been placed there.

Early railroad office furnishings from the 1907 depot on display. (Photo by Diane Hardy.)

An issue of the Gam, *Beaufort's weekly newspaper, featuring an article by Nancy Russell and a photo of the rail bus. (Courtesy the* Gam.)

The Carolinian, Norfolk Southern's Rail Bus that serviced Beaufort from 1935-1937 in place of regular passenger trains

THE RAIL BUS

In 1935, after nearly 30 years of service by train, the Norfolk & Southern began using the rail bus for transportation from Goldsboro to Beaufort. Five days a week the rail bus would come to Beaufort, then turn north and go to Chocowinity, where one could connect to Norfolk.

During the Depression, rail buses were more economical and easier to operate than locomotives. Plus, the need for coal and water disappeared. The rail bus was just about what it sounds like: a bus that ran on the rails of the former train engines. Nearly 60 feet long, they were made of lightweight aluminum and steel and had room for more than 50 passengers, baggage, and mail.

The bus was operated by gasoline, as automobiles were, and were luxuriously appointed with comfortable seats, heat, bathrooms, and a water cooler. The staff included an engineer, a conductor who took up the tickets and called out the stops, and a porter who helped passengers with their baggage and with getting on and off.

Fares were reduced in 1937 to 1.5¢ per mile, with half fare for children under 12. Some time in the same year, the service was ended. Bus travel was most likely the next connector of Beaufort to the outside world, as well as the new airport that had been established in the 1930s.

GROCERY SHOPPING THE OLD-FASHIONED WAY

In Beaufort there were several small grocery stores and four of them, Charlie Hill's, Potter's, Ikie Moore's, and C.D. Jones, were located in one block of downtown. Nancy Russell wrote primarily about the C.D. Jones Grocery, which is related here.

C.D. Jones opened in 1913 on the water side of Front Street. A family-owned and -operated grocery store, it was the largest of all the Front Street stores, with a lift that was originally pulled by hand to take merchandise to the third floor for storage. The first commercial refrigeration in town was in C.D. Jones's store. Fresh produce from local farmers was available, including seasonal vegetables like collards, sweet potatoes, red potatoes, green beans, squash, cabbage, and tomatoes. The store also carried dried mullet roe and had live chickens for sale.

Christopher Delamar Jones, the son of Thomas Redding Jones who was lost at sea, founded the store. He had served as collector of customs until being replaced when Woodrow Wilson was elected president. C.D. died in 1924, and his son-in-law C.Z. Chappell managed the store until 1931, when C.D.'s son Paul took the reins. Another son John served as the meat manager, and a third son Christopher (Crip) helped run the operation. The boys' sister Mildred was the bookkeeper.

Beaufort's teenage boys worked as delivery boys, including Bert Brooks, now the owner and operator of Brooks Funeral Home, another family-operated business; Gehrmann Holland Jr., who was to become the sheriff one day; Tommy Potter, a Beaufort mayor; and Henry Safrit of the Safrit Lumber Company.

A view of Front Street in the 1940s showing the C.D. Jones grocery store. (Courtesy Beaufort Historical Association.)

Part of Front Street, in the 1930s.

Deliveries were sometimes made two or three times a day to the same house. Cecil Sewell was the delivery truck driver who would load up the mail orders and take off with his sister Kathryn along for company, driving all the way to Harkers Island and downeast making deliveries.

Shopping at C.D. Jones's grocery store, like the others in town, was an experience we no longer have in these days of large, do-it-yourself shopping centers. From the early 1900s through 1960, there were two ways to place an order: in person or through a delivery boy who came to the house. Either way, the grocery list was written up, filled, and delivered by local young men riding on one of the many bicycles owned by the store. If you were one of the few people who owned a car, you would merely drive up to the front door, toot the horn, and have your order taken and filled. Once phones arrived, they became a popular way to order groceries.

The stores were always kept in spic-and-span condition. Before opening, the sidewalks were swept, the windows were washed, the awnings were lowered, and the bicycles were ready to go. Fruits and vegetables were arranged in baskets out front under the window. On warm days, the doors were opened at both the water side and the street side to allow the breezes to blow through from Taylor's Creek. There were screened doors to keep the pests away and fans to help circulate the air. On cold days, the stove was cranked up, and one could get warm and cozy while shopping.

On Saturdays, the people who lived downeast would come by boat to shop in Beaufort. When the menhaden fleet was in, the boats would tie up near the store and purchase all their supplies locally. Items were weighed to order, either loose in a tray or in a basket or other type of container. Meats such as pork, beef, and poultry were kept in refrigerated cases. John Jones wore the meat manager's recognizable white hat and apron and kept sawdust on the floor. While customers waited, he would cut their meat to order. But if you were ordering a turkey for a holiday, it was best do that at least 30 days in advance.

DRUG STORES

In 1910 the drug store in Beaufort was Dr. Charles Duncan's. Frank Roland Bell, a young man who worked in the store, decided that it was to be his life's work. He went off to attend pharmacy school and returned in 1913 to work at the drug store. In 1917, he joined the army in the Medical Corps where he contracted tuberculosis. He then went to law school but didn't take the exam. He came back home to Beaufort and, in 1919, formed a partnership with Ivey Guthrie to open the Guthrie-Bell Drug Store. In 1926, he went on his own, starting Bell's Drug Store, which today is owned and operated by Lynwood Daughtry and Thomas Lilly.

Besides making up prescriptions and dispensing medicines, the drug store offered delivery by young teenagers on bicycles and curb service. You could also send and receive telegrams, or use the telephone that was made available to

Bell's Drug Store on Front Street. (Photo by Diane Hardy.)

The Soda Fountain on Middle Lane. (Photo by Diane Hardy.)

customers. Scales for checking your weight and your horoscope were located on the sidewalk, at a cost of 1¢.

The druggists wore tan jackets. Comic books abounded and peanuts were prepared by frying them in cooking oil, draining, salting, and packing them. But the most wondrous part of going to the drug store was the soda fountain. Tables and booths were available, and fountain cokes, fresh squeezed orangeade and lemonade, and milkshakes were all served with your "to order" homemade sandwich of ham, pimento cheese, or Lizzie Chadwick's chicken salad, toasted or not.

To top it off, there was ice cream by the cup or the cone. High school students worked on weekends and holidays as soda jerks. Beaufort is fortunate today to have a terrific re-creation of the original soda fountain, which is located on Middle Lane and known as The Soda Fountain. A taste of the past brings back memories of the long-gone drug store soda fountains.

Dr. Bell also helped fund the education of future pharmacists like Clarence Guthrie and David Jones, who opened their drug store in 1941. The first female pharmacist in Carteret County was Beaufort's own Evelyn Salter. All three drug stores in Beaufort took turns opening on Sundays after church. Bell's Drug Store was sold in 1969 and relocated to its present site at the corner of Turner and Front Streets in the 1970s during urban renewal.

FISH HOUSES AND FISHING

The lifeblood of Beaufort before the onset of tourism was the fishing industry. Fish houses were located in the 500 block of Front Street on Taylor's Creek, as well as on Town Creek at the end of Pine Street. By the end of the twentieth century, all these buildings had disappeared, having been torn down during urban renewal or fallen down from disuse.

Trawlers would dock on the creek to unload their catches of the day. Many of the boats were owned by fishermen from downeast or Salter Path on Bogue Banks. Seafood was shipped by train to Richmond, Washington, D.C., Baltimore, and New York City, or sold locally if there was a smaller catch. The Way Brothers Fish House, opened in 1913 at the east end of the block on the water side, was the first to sink during urban renewal.

Menhaden brought prosperity to Beaufort. Boats would come in the fall, dock along Front Street, and buy their groceries and fuel to get ready to go out. The fish factories came to life and the smell of cooking fish permeated the town when the wind blew in the right direction. Those who pinched their noses and made faces when that happened were told, "That is the smell of money!"

Menhaden products were shipped by rail for additional processing and packaging. There were several well-known factories, including the Harvey Smith plant at Gallants Point, the original site of Blade's, Doans, and C.P. Dey. It was

The menhaden fleet at the docks on Front Street. (Courtesy Beaufort Historical Association.)

Early menhaden boats tied up on Front Street. (Courtesy Beaufort Historical Association.)

the Dey plant at Lennoxville that was purchased by Standard Products and today is owned by a local conglomerate known as Beaufort Fisheries.

The Smith plants and boats ranged from Long Island to Louisiana, and it was the operation of Harvey Smith that provided long-term jobs for many of Beaufort's workers. Most of the employees were African-American men who worked the purse seine boats, hauled the huge nets onto the mother ship, and unloaded the boat at the processing plant. In 1972, Smith converted the Beaufort plant to seafood processing. The company's reign was over in 1976 at Smith's death. During the best years of the menhaden operations, hundreds of boats plied the waters of Taylor's and Town Creeks.

Several of the African-American fishermen rose to be captains, but the most memorable time of their work was when they would sing or chant while hauling in the nets. The chanteymen had a lead singer who would set the rhythm of the song, with the rest of the men singing as they pulled in the nets. The lead would answer, and the men would chant again. This continued until all the nets were aboard. In the 1980s, the remaining chanteymen were invited to perform at Carnegie Hall in New York City.

In the earlier days, many of the young men of the town would bravely climb to the top of the crow's nest on a shad boat and dive straight into Taylor's Creek. And this was in the winter, as that is the time the boats were in port. Today, in the late fall, it is a sight to behold the menhaden boats entering the inlet and making their way down Taylor's Creek to the Beaufort Fisheries plant.

AIR RAID
PRECAUTIONS & WARNING

In This Period Of Extreme Emergency It Is Very Necessary That Everyone Be As Familiar As Possible With All

Air Raid Warning Signals and Obey
Blackout Warning when given

The Warning For BLACKOUTS In Beaufort
Is As Follows:

A CONTINUOUS BLAST FROM SIRENS
Such As Fire Engine Type

FOR A PERIOD OF THREE MINUTES

The All Clear Signal Will Be 2 Ten Second Blasts From the Sirens
With A 5 Second Interval.

ORDINANCE

WHEREAS, the existence of a state of war between this country and certain foreign powers have precipitated an emergency in the country as a whole:

AND WHEREAS, such emergency demands the enactment of ordinances with respect to blackout regulations consistent and in conformity with requirements of national defense:

NOW, THEREFORE, BE IT RESOLVED:

Sec. 1. That such air raid warden or deputies as are or may hereafter be appointed by the duly constituted authorities be, and they are, vested with full power and authority of City Policemen acting in conjunction with and as auxiliary to the regular City Police Force. As such they shall have full power and authority to effect arrest and enforce rules and regulations which have been or may hereafter be prescribed and promulgated during the existence and growing out of the present emergency. They shall take the prescribed oath of office and be in

every respect subject to the powers and authorities under which their duties and responsibilities are conferred upon them.

Sec. 2. Whenever an air raid signal or signals shall be given by the regular and proper authorities, and whenever blackouts by the regular and proper authorities are ordered, all owners, proprietors and—or occupants of all residences, dwellings and places of business of every kind and character located within the municipality, and all owners and occupants of boats in the immediate harbor of Beaufort, shall blackout or cause to be blacked out all such residences, dwellings or places of business and boats; and such blackout shall remain until such time as the "all clear" signal shall have been given, or appropriate orders otherwise have been given for a lifting of the blackout, partial or total.

Sec. 3. Whenever any blackout signal or warning shall have been given, as above provided for, all operators of motor vehicles shall immediately turn out all lights on

such motor vehicle and bring them to a full stop against the unpainted curb in such manner and fashion as may be most conducive to the safety of operators and the public; and the lights on such motor vehicle shall not again be turned on until due and proper notice has been given of the lifting of said blackout order; that no vehicle shall be parked against the painted curb after sun-down.

Sec. 4. Any person, firm or individual violating any of the provisions of the foregoing ordinances shall for the first offense be fined $5.00, and for a second offense $30.00, and for a third or subsequent offense shall be committed to jail for not less than 30 days.

Read, passed and adopted by the Board of Commissioners of the Town of Beaufort, This 15 day of December, 1941.

G. M. PAUL, Mayor.

Attest:

Attest: T. M. THOMAS,
City Clerk.

An air raid warning, which ran in the local paper, to Beaufort citizens during World War II.

THE SECOND WORLD WAR

Stories abound of German submarines torpedoing oil tankers in the shipping lanes off the North Carolina coast. Houses shook, dishes rattled, there were oil slicks on the beaches and shorelines, and flames of burning ships could be seen offshore at night. Many of the wounded survivors were treated at the hospital in Morehead City where a special burn unit was annexed.

Other rumors told of people living downeast and on Bogue Banks sending signals to the German ships off the coast, but nothing was ever proven. And still others say that some of the German sailors even managed to come ashore and decided to stay in the county and build new lives for themselves.

It was also during this time that the marine base at Cherry Point became a pivotal point for the protection of the coast and the country. Personnel were moved into the area and new houses were built in Beaufort to assist in their relocation and provide a spurt of growth for the town.

THE BEAUFORT HISTORICAL ASSOCIATION

After the war, many of the residents of Beaufort, along with civic and religious groups, realized the historical importance of the state's third-oldest town. It was at this time that the first major restoration was undertaken in what is known today as the Old Burying Ground on Ann Street.

At about the same time as the first restorations, the Beaufort Historical Association (BHA) was beginning to emerge. Members of the Beaufort Woman's Club decided to open their homes for tours by the attendees. In 1960, the BHA was officially founded. Since it was 251 years after the founding of the town in 1709, Beaufort celebrated its 251st anniversary, which further ignited interest in history and restoration. This led to the decision to hold an annual celebration.

The purpose of the BHA was and continues to be "to utilize Beaufort's historic background to the fullest to promote summer tourist trade." Membership fees were established and committees were formed to look into long-term plans and ways to finance future projects. Among these were a plan for a museum to house artifacts donated for display in the old county jail building, now located on the grounds; a museum of the sea that was already established on the waterfront; a reenactment of the 1747 pirate invasion; and continuing tours of historic landmarks.

In 1962, a prototype of the present plaque was presented to the membership and approved for use in recognizing historic structures, and the old county jail was set aside by the county commissioners to be used as a museum of collected artifacts. By 1963, 20 buildings were wearing plaques indicating their name and date of construction, and the first antiques show was scheduled to be sponsored by the BHA. The annual tour of homes was continued by the Beaufort Woman's Club until 1980, when the BHA took the reins.

The BHA worked diligently to raise funds. Brochures were created to promote the organization and properties were acquired, including the two Bell houses

The BHA plaque found on Beaufort homes 100 years or more old. (Photo by Diane Hardy.)

located in their original setting. The adjacent land was purchased and other buildings, such as the Leffers cottage, Apothecary shop, and Old Jail were moved to the historic site. The 1796 courthouse, moved to the site in the 1970s, has recently undergone a two-year restoration process, converting it back to what it was when originally built.

Nationally and internationally known, the BHA's historic site is visited annually by more than half a million visitors. From every state in the union they come by car, van, bus, and cruise ship to see history recreated. The association has also continued to offer the Old Homes Tour each summer during the last weekend in June, most recently adding some of the spectacular gardens of the local citizenry.

URBAN RENEWAL

Also in the 1960s, the voters of Beaufort made the decision to renew the waterfront side of Front Street between Turner and Queen Streets. Most of the buildings that had been the lifeblood of the community were dismantled or burned to make way for the newer ones that still exist today. Only one building remains from that time.

The BHA actively brings Beaufort's history to life. (Photo by Diane Hardy.)

An early postcard of Beaufort's waterfront showing the boardwalk. (Courtesy Beaufort Historical Association.)

The new boardwalk was built, with docks and piers for the many boats that ply the waters of the east coast between Maine and the Bahamas, a new dockhouse with a dock master was established, parking areas were laid out, a restaurant was built, and a building with several small shops and offices completed the project.

THE MARITIME MUSEUM

The museum's collection began in the late 1800s to represent North Carolina at the 1898 International Fisheries Expo in Norway. On return to the United States, the collection was displayed at the U.S. Fisheries Laboratory on Pivers Island in Beaufort. In 1959, funding and organization of the museum holding an even larger collection was delegated to the North Carolina Department of Agriculture, a branch of the North Carolina Museum of Natural History.

In 1975, the first full-time curator was appointed. Charles R. McNeill, former operations manager at the North Carolina Port in Morehead City, assumed the position of what was known at the time as the Hampton Mariners Museum. It was at this time that the emphasis on maritime history was added. Under the guidance of McNeill, with assistance from Jane Wolff, the museum officially opened its doors in rented space in the first block of Turner Street.

Over the years the collection of articles of maritime history, complete with wonderful, artistically designed displays and paintings of ships and coastal scenes grew in size, and the need for more room was soon apparent. In 1985, on land donated by Mrs. Harvey Smith, the present building was completed. The collection was transferred to the new facility along with Director McNeill and Jane Wolff.

Volunteers with an abiding interest in maritime and coastal natural history came to assist in greeting visitors, giving tours, and promoting the new North Carolina Maritime Museum.

Thirteen years after assuming the position of curator McNeill retired, having seen the museum grow into one of the nation's finest maritime museums. In 1972, under the direction of Rodney Barfield, the new director, the Watercraft Center on Taylor's Creek was completed. It is a large facility with huge doors on both the creek side and Front Street side, where anyone can feel the cool breezes when passing by, hear the sounds of workers creating a new boat, and smell the aroma of newly cut or shaved wood.

The North Carolina Maritime Museum continues to be recognized as a top-rated, nationally accredited, and internationally known maritime museum

The North Carolina Maritime Museum Watercraft Center on Front Street. (Photo by Diane Hardy.)

A drawing of the Hampton Mariner's Museum, the original site of the present-day North Carolina Maritime Museum on Turner Street, by the author.

offering programs year-round with lectures, field trips, and workshops for all ages. An added attraction in the past couple of years is the use of the museum as the repository for the artifacts from the *Queen Anne's Revenge*, the flagship believed to have belonged to Blackbeard, which was discovered in 1997 in the Beaufort Inlet.

PIRACY IN THE PRESENT

It should be known that Beaufort is the proud home of a present-day privateer known as Sinbad, who lives and sails aboard his ship *Meka II*.

In the mid-1970s, Ross Morphew, a.k.a. Sinbad, and his family sailed into town aboard his ship, which he had built while living in the Great Lakes region. He

A scene from Beaufort's early maritime history. (Courtesy Beaufort Historical Association.)

settled in, becoming the owner of the Spouter Inn, an eatery in the second block of Front Street, which still operates today.

In 1976, Sinbad and his crew participated in the tall ship gathering in New York to celebrate the 200th anniversary of the beginning of our nation. He continues to take part in maritime celebrations along the east coast, but he is best known for starting the "pirate invasion" tradition in Beaufort.

Memories of past invasions include the young men of the town climbing into a longboat with skull and crossbones on the front two sides, rowing down the cut toward the landing area, and being bombarded by water balloons from the citizenry in their small crafts. Following along was the *Meka II* with cannon blazing, making a sound that could be heard all the way to Town Creek.

A terrible battle would ensue between Sinbad and the volunteer militia, with the pirates finally landing and chasing the lovely young ladies who stood on the shore to watch. In earlier days, the pirates would then be captured by the militia and hauled away to jail in a cart with two huge wheels. Sinbad would eventually sail off into the sunset through the Beaufort Inlet.

The pirate invasion saw its demise in 1984 following the growth of the crowds, some members of which became unruly and disruptive. It was also another time of growth in Beaufort, and the part of Front Street between Queen and Pollock Streets where the invasion took place was being crowded with more docks and boats, and on the land side the new Inlet Inn was built.

A drawing of the Meka II, *Beaufort's "pirate" ship, by the author.*

151

EPILOGUE

Beaufort's streets, waterfront, and surrounding areas have not changed drastically since the early 1700s. Houses that were built in the eighteenth century on Front Street, particularly in the first and second block, are still standing today, occupied by families whose ancestors helped develop the town. Although Front Street is now paved, early on it was merely a path along the shore.

The government buildings are no longer in the middle of the third block as they were when Sauthier sailed along Taylor's Creek in 1770 and made his map of the town. Part of this block is occupied today by the North Carolina Maritime Museum.

The original buildings along the waterfront in the fourth and fifth blocks have been replaced with modern parking lots, restaurants, and gift shops. On the land side of Front Street in these two blocks are some of the nineteenth-century office buildings mixed with some newer structures. Only two of the several houses that occupied space on the land side remain, the others having been torn down or moved to other locations.

One of the 1820s brick buildings on Turner Street remains, with another now located on the historic site of the Beaufort Historical Association. The original school and family lodging house of one of Beaufort's early teachers still stands majestically in the second block of Turner Street, just a few steps away from the brick edifice of the Odd Fellows Lodge.

The Methodist church begun at the time of the Revolution at the corner of Craven and Broad Streets and completed in the early nineteenth century is used today for services by the AME Zion church.

The "new" Methodist church on Ann Street, built on the corner south of the first one shortly before the onset of the War between the States, as well as the Episcopal church in the second block of Ann Street built at the same period, are still serving their congregants.

The cemetery called the Old Burying Ground, located in the fourth block of Ann Street and surrounded by three churches, is no longer available for burial except for members of those families who have ancestors there and space remaining. It has been preserved, restored, and protected by the town and the Beaufort Historical Association over the past many years. A place of quiet, tranquil beauty, the grounds are covered with live oaks and vines that have graced the spot for centuries.

The families who came, built, lived, and died in Beaufort continue today through their many descendants. Although many newcomers have moved to the area in the past 25 years, Beaufort is still a very unique and blessed place to live.

An early image of the Atlantic Hotel on Taylor's Creek. (Courtesy Beaufort Historical Association.)

APPENDIX
A BRIEF HISTORY OF BEAUFORT'S NAME

The history of the Beaufort family begins in the 1300s with the family of Edward III of England. During his reign, the House of Commons grew more powerful, as did criticism of the Church of England. By 1369, England was exhausted and disillusioned. The church claimed exemption from taxation and flaunted its wealth while ousting nobility from public office. The king was old and failing and there was a resurgence of baronial power.

One of Edward's sons was John of Gaunt, Duke of Lancaster, who set about to rebalance the power of the lords. In 1377, he and reformer John Wycliffe allied. Gaunt packed parliament while Wycliffe lent support, preaching against moral abuses. Hostility developed however, and eventually the partnership fell apart.

When Edward III died, his grandson Richard II, not yet 10 years old, became king. Gaunt was his uncle and as head of the Council of Regency ruled the land. Although there was a peasant revolt, the king and the royal judges had restored order. At age 20, Richard decided to be master of his council and escape control of his uncles, including Gaunt. The royal judges and the lords appellant put pressure on the king, and a bloody reprisal followed.

Gaunt's brother Thomas of Woodstock, Duke of Gloucester, along with other heads of a baronial hierarchy, denounced the chief justice as a traitor. Gaunt quit the realm to pursue interests abroad and left his son Henry to take charge of his royal estates and interests. In 1387 an armed force went to London but was met by the lords appellant and Henry, and was defeated. Richard was now in the hands of the faction that had usurped his rights.

In 1389, Richard took his seat on the council at age 23. Bishop Thomas, the Earl of Arundel's brother, surrendered the great seal on demand, and Bishop Gilbert quit the treasury. When John of Gaunt returned from Spain, Henry reconciled with the king. For eight years the king tolerated Arundel and Gloucester.

Richard's wife, Anne of Bohemia, died in 1394. In 1396, he married Isabelle, daughter of France's Charles VI. He went to Ireland, raised an army, allied with France, and began to construct a court party. Gaunt, his son, and Mowbray, Earl of Norfolk, a former appellant, rallied to the King partly because of their hostility to Arundel and Gloucester.

Richard had Arundel declared a traitor and beheaded. Gloucester was arrested, taken to Calais, and murdered. Henry and Richard's relationship deteriorated. Henry felt he had saved Richard's life in 1388, and he accused Mowbray of treason when he voiced his opinion about the king's feelings of the former appellants. The king exiled Mowbray for life and Henry for a decade. Mowbray died, but Henry lived in France and schemed.

In 1399, John of Gaunt died and Henry succeeded to his vast estates. Richard, needing money, seized these estates and disinherited his cousin Henry. The king then left for Ireland. Henry went to England to claim his lawful estates. The king returned and realized he was beaten, so he submitted to Henry who was now in command of the whole administration. Richard was put in the tower and Henry ascended to the throne as Henry the IV, or Henry of Bolingbroke.

Henry's eldest son, Henry Prince of Wales, became very active in state business as his father's health declined and he was pressed by his half uncles, the three Beaufort brothers, to take over. The king died in 1413 and Henry V became king at age 26. In 1420, he married Catherine, daughter of Charles VI of France, and became known as king of England and heir of France. He died in 1422 and the crown passed to his son, an infant of nine months. Charles VI of France also died and the baby became king of France as well.

Gaunt's grandsons Bedford and Gloucester were the uncles of the new king and became his protectors. John, Duke of Bedford, brother of Henry V, went to France as regent and commander in chief. The Duke of Gloucester, brother of Bedford and Henry V, became protector of the baby king. Gloucester married Jacqueline, Princess of Hainault, Holland, and Zeeland.

Henry VI was crowned in Paris in 1431 at age 10. At 15 he was attending council meetings and by 18 had founded his colleges at Eton and Cambridge. Bedford died in 1435 and tension grew between Gloucester and Cardinal Beaufort, the Bishop of Winchester; and William de la Pole, Earl of Suffolk.

In 1441, Henry VI turned against the Duke of Gloucester by attacking his new wife. At 23, Henry was to marry. Each of the Lancastrian factions wanted to provide him a queen but Cardinal Beaufort, with his brothers and ally Suffolk, prevailed over Gloucester. Suffolk arranged a marriage with Margaret of Anjou, niece of the king of France, and Henry was married in 1445.

Suffolk and Edmund Beaufort, nephew of the cardinal, arrested Gloucester when he came to parliament. Beaufort, now the Duke of Somerset, became commander of the army in France, while Suffolk stayed home. The army was defeated and Edmund took the blame.

Claims of opposition to the House of Lancaster were embodied in Richard, Duke of York, who had a prior right to the crown. He was the son of Richard, Earl of Cambridge and grandson of Edmund, Duke of York, a younger brother of John of Gaunt. Richard was the great grandson of Edward III and the only other person besides Henry VI with an unbroken male descent from Edward III. He also had claim in the female line through descent of Gaunt's older brother Lionel of Clarence.

BIBLIOGRAPHY

Barbour, Ruth P. *History of the Beaufort Historical Association January 25, 1960–January 1, 1990*. Beaufort: Beaufort Historical Association, 1990.

Beaufort Historical Association. *Beaufort, North Carolina, "By the Sea."* Beaufort: Beaufort Historical Association, 1940.

Butler, Jon. *Becoming America, The Revolution Before 1776*. Cambridge, MA: Harvard University Press, 2000.

Crow, Jeffrey J. *A Chronicle of North Carolina During the American Revolution 1763–1789*. Raleigh, NC: North Carolina Department of Cultural Resources, Division of Archives and History, 1975.

Cumming, William P. *Mapping the North Carolina Coast, Sixteenth-Century Cartography and the Roanoke Voyages*. Raleigh, NC: North Carolina Department of Cultural Resources, Division of Archives & History, 1988.

Davis, David Brion & Steven Mintz. *The Boisterous Sea of Liberty, A Documentary History of America From Discovery Through the Civil War*. New York, NY: Oxford University Press, 1998.

Davis, Maurice. *History of the Hammock House and Related Trivia*. Beaufort: Beaufort Historical Association, 1984.

Hardy, Diane, Mamré Wilson, and Marilyn Collins. Images of America: *Beaufort's Old Burying Ground, North Carolina*. Charleston, SC: Arcadia Publishing, 1999.

History of North Carolina. Raleigh, NC: North Carolina Department of Education.

Hulton, Paul. *America 1585, The Complete Drawings of John White*. Chapel Hill, NC: University of North Carolina Press, 1984.

Keen, M.H. *Beaufort family in England in the Later Middle Ages*. Grolier, 1973.

Lawson, John. *A New Voyage to Carolina*. Chapel Hill, NC: University of North Carolina Press, 1967.

Marshall, P.J., ed. *The Oxford History of the British Empire, The Eighteenth Century*. New York, NY: Oxford University Press, 1998.

Miller, Helen Hill. *Passage to America*. Raleigh, NC: North Carolina Department of Cultural Resources, 1983.

Morison, Samuel Eliot. *The European Discovery of America, The Northern Voyages, A.D. 500–1600*. New York, NY: Oxford University Press, 1971.

Neal, Georgia W. *The Old Topsail Inlet, A Story of Old & New Beaufort*. Beaufort:

Beaufort Historical Association, 1937.

Perdue, Theda. *Native Carolinians, The Indians of North Carolina*. Raleigh, NC: North Carolina Department of Archives and History, 1985.

Powell, William S. *The North Carolina Gazetteer, A Dictionary of Tar Heel Places*. Chapel Hill, NC: University of North Carolina Press, 1968.

Robinson, Melville. *Riddle of the Lost Colony*. New Bern, NC: Owen G. Dunn, 1946.

Russell, Nancy. "Beaufort Scrapbook." The *Gam*. 1999–2001.

Williams, Basil. "Carteret, John, 1st Earl of Granville." *A Contrast in Contemporaries*. Grolier, 1943.

Wilson, Mamré Marsh. A Brief History of Beaufort and Carteret County, North Carolina, Beaufort: 1998.

———. *A Researcher's Journal, Beaufort, North Carolina and the Civil War*. New Bern, NC: 1999.

Wolff, Jane. "Humble Beginnings—Exciting Future." *Waterline*. Beaufort: North Carolina Maritime Museum. 1997.

Inside Fort Macon · Atlantic Beach · NC

A drawing of the inside of Fort Macon in Atlantic Beach, North Carolina, by the author.

INDEX

An early twentieth-century tourist brochure for Beaufort. (Courtesy Beaufort Historical Association.)